Eternal Life

and how to enjoy it

Eternal Life

and how to enjoy it

88
110
129 *111*
167 ←
172 ←
145
167

a first-hand account

GORDON PHINN

HAMPTON ROADS
PUBLISHING COMPANY, INC.
for the evolving human spirit

Cover design by Marjoram Productions
Cover digital imagery © 2004 Corbis and PhotoSearch/Image Library
Author portrait by Colin Cherry

Hampton Roads Publishing Company, Inc.
1125 Stoney Ridge Road
Charlottesville, VA 22902

434-296-2772
fax: 434-296-5096
e-mail: hrpc@hrpub.com
www.hrpub.com

If you are unable to order this book from your local
bookseller, you may order directly from the publisher.
Call 1-800-766-8009, toll-free.

Library of Congress Cataloging-in-Publication Data

Phinn, Gordon.
  Eternal life and how to enjoy it : a first-hand account / [channeled
through] Gordon Phinn.
    p. cm.
  ISBN 1-57174-408-8 (5 1/2 x 8 1/2 tp : alk. paper)
  1. Spirit writings. 2. Future life. I. Phinn, Gordon. II. Henry
(Spirit) III. Title.
  BF1301.H44 2004
  133.9'3--dc22
                                        2004007800

10 9 8 7 6 5 4 3 2 1

Printed on acid-free paper in the United States

Preface

I have been associating with Gordon for 20-odd years Earth time. I met him initially when he was out here visiting with his recently deceased father. The father had brought him along to one of my talks and he stayed behind to ask some questions about karma he'd obviously been sweating over for some time.

In our ensuing discussion I was impressed with his determination to unmask the subtleties of cause and effect, which in essence are multidimensional—i.e., operate in all directions at once. I recall using the old "pebble thrown in a pool" metaphor but expanding the pool to a sphere moving through time, and the ripples moving three-dimensionally outwards from a point of impact—when he suddenly disappeared, back to the world of the waking, no doubt to relieve a bulging bladder.

The next time he found me we began an intermittent series of instructional visits, in which I put him through the usual paces for training out-of-body helpers.

In no time at all, I had him sinking to the bottom of turbulent rivers, flying through the infernos of forest fires, battling all manner of demons in thought-form land, breaking bread with religionists of all shapes and forms, and practicing kindness with all ugly strangers.

He is not my only student, and by no means my best, but as he is a writer willing to risk his literary reputation by being tarred with the brush of channeling, we decided he was the perfect scribe for the task we have undertaken.

Which is?

An easily accessible account of life in the spirit planes, updating the rather too religious testimonies of classic spiritualism, and expanding the useful but still fragmentary accounts of the recent NDE and OBE literature.

Gordon has been sitting here with me these last few moments as I express these thoughts. He chuckles, knowing he'll have to write them all down later. I send the thought forms in his direction and they hover about his apartment, waiting to be picked up and entered into the memory of his old computer.

At first he tells me how much fun he's having writing the opening chapter, "First Day Dead." He'd been working on other sections on and off for months, losing then regaining his confidence. But all along he'd had a nagging sensation that he needed an opening, something simple and straightforward that people could walk into and admire, like a commodious hotel lobby.

Then one day at work he had a flash of how it could be. When he got home that evening he plugged right into the images I'd projected of my transition. Unlike Audrey, whom you will meet later, and with whom I processed words, I'd transmitted only pictures, basically as an experiment, but also to give him some kind of leeway, as he is after all a writer and needs to feel he is contributing in a creative way.

I ask him if he's telling friends about the project. Apparently so. For some he related it to seeing the popular movie *Ghost*. He told them it inspired him to gather together two decades of vivid dreams and thread them into some kind of narrative. Then he realized large chunks of intuition would be necessary to pave over the gaps in his memory. And if some choose to call that intuition channeling then who was he to interfere with their free will?

And the straw that broke the camel's back, as it were, was that out-of-body experience in which I escorted him up through the planes to the formless worlds of pure energy where he might experience one of the highest vibrations possible for those yet incarnate. We laugh as he tells me his Earthly self was not sure who conducted his trip. We laugh because we know how hard it is to carry through the consciousness of one's astral experience. The poor guy, he wanders around his daily life knowing he had a full slate the previous night but is barely able to recall any of it. He says it's the most frustrating thing. To illustrate, he is going to copy out his original 5 A.M. scribble of the trip.

> I go for this tremendous multidimensional trip with this character called Manlow or Manlove that completely blows my mind. He's part of some sort of psychic air force that takes willing people on these tours.
>
> Then I think I'm telling people about it and writing down details, and *that* turns out to be a dream. I get up and write this down and think about phoning SJ in England.
>
> The memories fade fast, but I felt in the "post-trip-but-still-dream" stage that it was ten times more mind blowing than any mere astral travel and that I was indeed very lucky. The guy Manlove was a cross (dig this) between James Dean and Jesus Christ, an extremely cool multidimensional tripster.
>
> This was a short journey of Robert Monroe spectacularity, no mere jaunt around the neighborhood. I only wish I hadn't

fooled myself by dreaming I was writing it down, because then the memories were even fresher. Now it's fading fast.

"What the hell was all that?" (He said stunned.)

We agree this would be an interesting addition to the text, even though it is but an approximation of the original, shall we say, rapture.

He tells me he wants to make the work more inclusive of others' experiences and mentions two recent friends who are currently recalling their soul rescue work. They are working with the Hemi-Sync tapes developed by Robert Monroe and using the reception area popularized by his work and known to his disciples as the Park. And these are only the most recent. There's also a woman from England whom he met, as he laughingly says, quite by synchronous circumstance, who works with methods originating in Brazil.

I tell him—why not? Surely diversity can only enrich. He asks if he should include his English friend's experiences of rescuing souls from military installations. She couldn't remember it too clearly, but he sensed she might have been misled by deceitful forces, as her innate kindliness sometimes borders on naiveté.

I admit that dark forces can be served by psychic spying and sundry forms of black magic pursued by the military, but remind him that a pure heart can only increase the level of light in any atmosphere.

Then I ask about his own recent nighttime work: How's it going? Well, the poor black man killed in an auto accident couldn't seem to stop worrying about his children long enough to be rescued, and the four drug smugglers are still in that bar in Mexico drinking to their health and laughing about their great getaway, even though their bullet-to-the-temple bodies lie rotting in a remote shack and the drugs are long gone to a rival's base. He shared a couple of rounds of thought-form tequila with them but they just didn't seem to give a shit. In fact two of them had just shared a thought-form hooker and seemed mighty pleased with their performance. As one of them argued,

"Buddy, if I'm so goddamn dead, how come I can get the biggest, longest-lasting boner of my life in there?"

I tell Gordon not to get discouraged. He laughs and says he's more amused than anything, but that's his basic temperament anyway. Which, of course, makes him well suited for the position. Bleeding hearts are no good here. That conventional sense of tragedy is just a burden in this line of work.

PART ONE

FIRST DAY DEAD

A Boring No-Account Accountant

I died in the early 1960s, during that breathing space between the Cuban missile crisis and the Kennedy assassination, those halcyon days of our commonwealth whose charm and promise have come to be commemorated, even by the cynical, as Camelot.

Indignant and dismayed by my wife's defection into the arms of my oldest rival, I did the previously unthinkable: called in sick to work and jumped into the car for an unscheduled weekend touring Pennsylvania.

A boring, no-account accountant she called me, and by God she was right, but I wasn't about to admit it then. It took about two years (Earth time) in Heaven to face the embarrassing truth.

Lovely September weather, and in that most appealing of northeastern states, I took the roads as they came, using whim of the moment as my map. Second day out, with the evening just stretching its intentions, I slammed head-on into a Ford of partying teenagers.

First Brush with Flight

Seconds probably passed, but all I knew was that I was suddenly hovering above, amazed and unbelieving, watching three of them crawl from the wreckage. Broken little children, forever bruised. The sight, so full of anguish and pain, pushed me to tears, something completely out of character for old Henry.

"It's about time," said a voice from my left.

I twisted to see a quite ordinary middle-aged man in golfing attire. He seemed bemused.

"I thought you were never going to cry, Mr. Cool-as-a-cucumber."

I felt mocked, yet I wasn't entirely sure. And I still hadn't a clue why I was hovering above the car. But I did manage to find some shreds of humor.

"I'll take that that as a compliment, if you don't mind."

"Be my guest, Henry. After all, I've been yours all these years." He nodded to the blue yonder. "Shall we, ah, be off then?"

Moving into the empty space above the fields and trees seemed quite pointless and yet somehow intriguing. I looked at him more closely. A balding golfer without clubs: There must've been at least ten just like him at the office. As golf mad as the younger ones were girl crazy. I copied his nod.

"What about down there?"

"That's okay, they're taken care of."

I looked down to see two rather waiflike women hovering over the wreckage. As I watched, one of them somehow, with a curling action not unlike smoke from a pipe, disappeared into it, reappearing seconds later with one of the boys, now strangely vibrant. I turned to the golfer, now grinning like a rather pompous sales manager at a month-end meeting.

"Are you people angels?"

"You might say that. We try to help out when we're needed."

"And you're going to take me to Heaven now?"

He took something out of his pocket and slipped it into his mouth. It could have been a mint. He didn't offer me one and I immediately wished he had. I'd always liked mints and I did feel kind of parched.

"Well, it's not exactly Heaven. It's more like orientation week at college."

"What, you mean lots of pretty girls and beer?" For a dead guy I thought that was pretty funny, but my golfing buddy showed no signs of amusement.

"Plenty of the former but not so much of the latter where we're going."

I shuddered at the thought of the abstemious vision of the afterlife held by my deeply puritan parents, only some of the luggage I left at home decades before.

"And golf too, I suppose?"

He smirked. "Only on the lower levels, I'm afraid."

Baffled, I allowed myself to be hand-held and whisked through space, rather like some mysterious boyhood shopping trip with my mother. At first we were flying over beautiful Pennsylvania, but quickly it all became a blur, then black, then very, very bright.

Suburban Connecticut

When my eyes became adjusted we were walking in a small park in suburban Connecticut. At least that's what it looked like.

"This is the model for that," my golfing guide assured me, as if reading my thoughts. I nodded. I couldn't see any point in arguing with him. We stepped along brightly.

I could see what looked like a family grouping in a backyard adjoining the little park. Someone who could've been the father looked up and waved, as if I were a neighbor just back from vacation. Children darted about squealing. I winced inwardly: Noisy kids were not my cup of tea.

"They all died in a house fire three years ago. Some electrical thing. Seem happy enough now though."

I took in this information without comment. The houses, very well spaced by Connecticut standards, were ranch style and strikingly large, as if everyone had just been granted the same sized bank loan, using it to build dens big enough for a wedding banquet and yards big enough for a magazine spread.

I spied some ducks paddling serenely in a nearby pond and asked my guide if we might sit and watch them. The benches by the shore were pristine, with museum-quality carved armrests.

"Yes, they are lovely, aren't they. Woodworker who lives nearby. One of his hobbies."

"You're reading my thoughts, aren't you."

"Yes, and I've been reading them all your life."

"Taking notes for judgment day?" I thought, under the circumstances, that this was quite witty.

"Not at all, Henry. Just helping out where necessary. As per our arrangement."

"And what arrangement is this?"

"The one you made before you were born. Actually one of many."

I stared intently at the ducks. They looked as wise as the prophets. A thought appeared in my head: We have our share of the ancient wisdom. It was not until much later that I realized the source of this telepathic transmission. And probably just as well; at the time such a revelation would have tipped me over the edge. I turned to my guide and tried to formulate one question out of the many that tumbled through my brain.

"You're telling me I was a person before I was a baby?"

"You bet."

"And you were there?"

"That's correct."

"And I asked you to read my thoughts?"

"No, not exactly. Your advisory panel suggested me for a guardian spirit and when you came to me with the idea I accepted. After all, you'd done an exemplary job for me in prerevolutionary France and post-Civil War Virginia; it was the least I could do."

"So I asked you to be my guardian angel and you've been floating around me all these years?"

"Well, from time to time. Say, would you like a mint?"

"I thought you'd never ask."

He reached into his pocket and handed me one. It was, by far, the mintiest mint I'd ever tasted. Transcendentally minty.

"Henry, don't imagine me as interfering at every opportunity; that's not how we operate. We help out from time to time. We give little nudges, to help you with the complexity of choices. And it's not the nudges so much as the timing of them."

I gazed at the ducks, hoping that I wouldn't hear any more voices in my head. My guide did not interrupt this pensive moment, a small grace I was initially grateful for, but as the seconds turned into minutes, I changed my tune.

"Perhaps you'd like to explore the neighborhood a bit, hmm?" He stood up encouragingly. I followed suit.

We ambled through the park and out onto a soil-covered thoroughfare lined with shade trees. A leafy suburban street minus the concrete and asphalt.

"Not really necessary here," muttered my host. I nodded knowingly.

We must've passed half a dozen sumptuous homes when I began to hear something more than a breeze rustling leaves. Some botanical gardens appeared to our left. I thought I could hear music, and I asked my guide if we might walk in.

He grinned, "Why, I thought you'd never ask."

We strolled along winding pathways surrounded by breathtakingly elegant floral displays. Praise seemed superfluous. And the fragrances! At the time I was overwhelmed. Now I would say something like: If one's nostrils were a palette, one could produce a work of art.

Turning past some voluminous flowering bushes I could not put a name to, we sighted the source of the music. A small opalescent band shell with an audience of thirty or forty sprawled on the grass in front. And on the stage a chamber group playing a Schubert octet.

I turned to my host. "Well, now I know I'm in Heaven!"

He smirked. "We aim to please."

"You knew I loved Schubert, of course."

"Certainly. We could've turned another way and heard some Elizabethan lute or some Dixieland jazz, but I felt confident this would be your choice."

We joined the audience at its edge. A couple of faces turned to smile. The atmosphere was very picniclike: blankets and baskets, apples with bites out of them.

Although I knew the piece well, having heard it in recital many times, I let myself just float away on the harmonies. In the midst of this little bliss an unwelcome thought bubbled up and I turned to my host and whispered, "How long have I been dead?"

"About fifteen minutes, I should reckon."

I couldn't honestly say that this surprised me more than anything else. I wish I could; being able to focus in on a couple of elements might have made it easier to swallow. As it was I just put aside my incredulity and enjoyed the moment for what it was.

Because of what I assumed was a natural iridescence coming from the structure of the band shell itself, it took me some time to distinguish the color show created by the music.

Streams of blue, green, purple, and gold curled around and about each other, creating fantastic spiraling patterns that mutated second by second, each abstract weave as wonderful as the last. I was dumbfounded and wondered how many more priceless moments were about to accumulate in my brief but brimming postmortem existence.

(And although the development of laser-beam technology on Earth has shown recent concert audiences some spectacular displays, the very nature of the physical plane does not permit the simultaneous expression of sound and light that is intrinsic to astral experience. But of course I had no notion of this on the day I died.)

In the midst of all this I was suddenly gripped by the notion that perhaps, after all, I was just dreaming, and I should really be taking notes on all the marvels to remind myself in the morning.

"Don't worry," whispered my guide, "everyone feels that way at first. This may seem too good to be true, but I assure you, it will all be here later for your repeated perusal, after we get you settled."

The Schubert came to an end; the crowd let out a collective sigh, and everyone seemed to be smiling. As the musicians prepared another piece, which I somehow knew was going to be Mozart, we stood up and sauntered off.

As we skirted the edge of the small crowd, I couldn't help but notice how beautiful all the women seemed. Before we'd made our quiet escape, I think I'd fallen in love about four times. My guide was good enough not to comment.

He asked if I'd care to visit the guest house. I couldn't see why not.

"Is that where they put up all the dead people?"

"You're catching on, Henry. Say, do you want a bath with power jets or just a shower?"

This was years before Jacuzzis, so all I could muster was, "You mean I get a choice?"

"Well it depends on how many people have passed over in the last couple of days. If there's been a train wreck or a ferry disaster you're screwed. 'Course you can always sleep on the lawn, it's so perfectly warm here."

"What about the bugs?"

"They're aren't any. At least not around here. They have their own sphere."

I did not really take in this last remark, as I could see we were approaching a mansion set in its own rather grand grounds. An estate, in fact. I actually wondered for a moment if he'd made a mistake. As usual he picked up my thought.

"If you'd prefer, there's always the Sunset Motel. A more, shall we say, egalitarian enterprise on the outskirts of town. You know, cheesy decor, wobbly furniture, and a chain-smoking couple called Fred and Edna who'll make you feel right at home."

I chuckled and kept walking.

The Guest House

Inside was what my parents would have called swanky, but to me it was more subdued than ostentatious. I felt refinement without pretension and activity without bustle.

The epitome of pretty desk clerks, who introduced herself as Phoebe, smoothly took over management of my immediate destiny. Jack, as she called him, excused himself, promising to seek me out later for refreshments. I thanked him for all his efforts on my behalf. I didn't believe in half of what he said, but life, that rapidly receding memory, had shown me there is never any harm in courtesy. Let's face it, I was just like some anxiety-prone agnostic who prays to St. Peter just in case. Phoebe said I was in luck: As there had been no major transitions, as she called them, there were several suites vacant, all with lovely views. If I cared to follow her, she'd give me a sample. Since I'd been smitten on contact, I contrived to keep her talking. Major transitions were, she responded, a challenge. Many needed a more hospital-like atmosphere, where their lifelong trust in the medical profession could be effectively used in their rebalancing, as she called it. Only some were like me, moving quickly from bewildered to bemused. I took her at her word.

We looked at a succession of rooms, each imaginatively appointed. I decided on the one with the most restful wallpaper. Perhaps I thought I needed to calm down. As I was examining the breathtaking view, sloping meadows leading to a series of lily ponds, one of which catered to a family of swans, Phoebe asked if Jack had been up to his old tricks.

I chuckled, saying I'd wondered about the golfing outfit. Apparently he was fond of sportswear, but had brought people in wearing all manner of outfits.

"You mean he's not just my guardian angel?"

"Oh no, he handles lots of transitions. It's one of his favorite hobbies as it gives him endless opportunities to be a teaser. He's probably out there right now, dolled up as a rabbi for some Jewish stroke victim, or a baseball hero for some teenage suicide. He does a fabulous Roosevelt impersonation."

I assumed she intended Franklin and then found myself wondering about national security issues. "Is that sort of thing allowed?"

"Oh, it's all in a good cause, no one minds. Now there's some clothes in the closet. A couple of suits if you really feel the need, but I think you'll find casual wear works best here. There's a lounge downstairs just off the lobby if you'd like company and refreshments, but may I be so bold as to suggest a nap first? You've been through a lot today."

"I'll say." I wanted to ask her for a date, but the very idea was just too absurd, so I thanked her for all the gracious help. She declared it her pleasure, helping people get settled, and she never tired of it.

She turned at the door. "Oh yes, I forgot. Here's a message left at the desk for you. The gentleman said he was once your grandfather."

I tried not to grimace. I didn't want to spoil her afternoon. That old blowhard, he was the last person I wanted to see.

The confused exhilaration I felt then, alone in that lovely suite, I still find impossible to describe. Although I'd read a couple of spiritual-type books in my college days, I had found them piously cloying and sentimental, not at all to my taste, and thus had forgotten their descriptions of postmortem bliss.

They had both been at pains to point out that the afterlife was for everyone, and not some church-going elect, but after all their efforts, it still seemed as though Heaven were reserved for goody-goodies. It never seemed like the sort of place you could see Charlie Parker playing to an audience of hopped-up hipsters. And as the Bird was my all-time hero at that point, I couldn't imagine being any place without him.

And although I had rather forsaken my jazz roots for the altogether more acceptable classics, I just could not see Heaven as then described. How could people be that continually nice? Well, Phoebe seemed to manage it. Maybe everyone else could too. I'd soon find out. But I couldn't help thinking how a little bit of deceit and smarminess spiced things up a bit.

Do the Dead Dream?

Eventually, responding to sheer curiosity as much as Phoebe's suggestion, I lay down on the bed. It was almost frighteningly comfortable. I actually felt a twinge of anxiety lying there. A residual conventionality raised me up to disrobe. Folding my clothes in a neat pile was second nature, I was not about to stop now.

Under the impeccably soft and cool sheets, I found myself wondering whether dead people dream. Would the existence of dreams prove one thing or another? Maybe I was dreaming now. Maybe, just maybe, if I went to sleep I could wake up into my old life. It sounds mad now but it sounded like a plan at the time.

Certainly, losing consciousness was no problem. I slept like a baby, and I have no idea for how long. All I know is I moved through warm darkness undisturbed and was delivered safely to the light of my opened eyes.

I lay there, feeling marvelously rested but probing for some vestige of dream memory, but nothing seemed willing to surface. Reluctantly,

I washed and dressed as if readying for a normal day. I watched myself go through the motions. Well, it was my first morning dead, maybe it took some practice to develop new habits. I stood by the window with the wonderful view. It looked morning-ish; no one seemed to be around. Even the swans seemed to have taken shelter.

A Face from the Past

I looked at the door to my room, realizing that I would have to open it at some point. This got me thinking about Rip Van Winkle and his hundred-year sleep, but my reveries were interrupted by a knock at the door.

Suspecting a maid on her rounds, I called out a come in. But it was my old college roommate Ben, looking so much like his old self I momentarily doubted my sanity.

"Ben, my God, what are you doing here?"

He walked towards me grinning. "Oh, I just thought I'd come by and say hello. You feeling fit?"

We shook hands with the same old vigor. "Never better. This dying stuff's a real tonic."

"Yes, remarkable isn't it? You could've knocked me over with a feather when I first passed."

"The heart finally give out?"

"Sure. It was inevitable, really. I was lucky to get 32 years with my condition. I'm just glad I didn't marry."

"Well, you're not missing much. For me it was about six months of true love followed by five years of fighting."

"Gee, I'm sorry to hear that."

"Don't be. I'm thrilled it's over. And I'm starting to see that this is much easier than divorce. Say, how long you been dead?"

"Just about a year, Earth time, although I'll tell you now that only feels like a few weeks here."

"Really."

"Yes. And things are such a gas here it's very much a case of time flies when you're having fun."

Suddenly I wondered how he knew I was here. Seems Jack, my golfing buddy and general factotum, had approached him to show me around, as the gulf between me and my grandparents would tend to magnify my discomfort rather than ease it. And as this arrangement was no more miraculous than anything else so far, I embraced it immediately.

I quickly accepted Ben's kind offer of a neighborhood tour. After a breakfast fit for a king, on which I unabashedly gorged and Ben merely nibbled, we ambled out onto the grounds.

My day was a perfect delight. I could write a book about it. Maybe one day I will. Strolling, swimming, sailing, socializing. A trip to the community center: a town hall, a school, day care, two theatres, craft and clothing boutiques, cafes, but no fire hall. There was absolutely no need for one, Ben assured me, but he did know of places where some had been set up as museums. The people who strolled throughout the town seemed chipper and cheerful. I remarked on the vacation-spot atmosphere. Ice cream cones were much in evidence.

One incident stands out. Sitting in one of the cafes, sipping a coffee that was so delicious I wondered aloud whether it had been brewed by angels, I saw a woman from my old neighborhood passing by. I was so shocked I called her name. We had been but passing acquaintances on Earth, passengers on the daily commute, but she seemed very pleased to see me, saying that no one else from the old town was here. We exchanged introductions and pleasantries, Ben politely allowing us to chatter.

Although both recent arrivals, she only eight days before me, our situations were otherwise quite different. She actually missed her family, two grown-up children and a husband, whereas I felt the severance of all my family ties to be something of a relief.

When I enquired how she coped she told me that her guide had kindly shown her how to descend closer to the Earth during their sleep times and communicate with them when they slipped out of body. I was intrigued: This was something new. Ben said he'd explain later.

Marcie said she was expected at the store, and on her invitation we accompanied her to a lovely craft shop, which seemed to do a brisk trade without any coin passing hands. Money was superfluous here, I was told, the artisans were happy just to see their work distributed. And of course the newly dead, accustomed to the old ways, were thrilled to get something for nothing.

On hearing that I was still at the guest house, Marcie invited me to visit her home whenever I felt like coming. She was just in the process of redecorating, and as the last tenant had such radically different taste she wouldn't mind getting some feedback on her progress. I said I'd be happy to oblige and it was arranged that I would come to the shop when I was ready.

The essential charm of this encounter was symptomatic of the kind of social interaction I experienced on arriving, although I must admit it took me some time to come to the realization.

I thought there'd be more important things to consider in Heaven than wallpaper and pictures, but in the middle astral, as I was to later come to call it, souls as yet unable to confront the burdens of immortality and eternity often resort to such concerns in great relief. After the endless struggles of Earth, many are happy just to bathe in the omnipresent bliss.

Feeling the Pull

Towards what I felt to be evening, I grew uneasy. About what, I couldn't tell. Ben inquired, was I feeling the pull? I said I was feeling something very powerful, but I didn't know what. He guided me to a secluded bench in yet another park and explained how the strong emotions of those on Earth who knew me would draw me like a magnet. He said it was best if I didn't resist and told me not to worry, that he would follow along wherever I went.

In the blink of an eye I was in a strange bedroom. My wife, Veronica, was under the covers with Reid, my old rival. I could feel the agony of our triangle but I had absolutely no idea what to do about it. Sweat, sex, grief, and consolation seemed to be the main elements.

Veronica was certainly stricken, but her sadness was driven by guilt more than love. Well, that was no surprise, we'd been battling for years and this was not the first time she'd fled to Reid. What did shock me was how I felt her emotions so directly, as if I were hot-wired to her heart. Quite disturbing for a cool cat like me.

Then I was at my parents' place. Mother was standing in my old bedroom, quietly sobbing. My father was downstairs making phone calls. Once again I'd caught him at a bad time. Couldn't I have waited another month when the London office would be up and running on its own?

And suddenly another shift. I was in the office, at the doorway to the lunchroom. Two women were hugging and crying. One was my secretary, Elaine. She seemed terribly distraught and I couldn't think why. She had been so calmly efficient for so long. Then I realized it was me she was grieving for. She had secretly loved me and I had never noticed. She actually said as much to Lucille, so I knew I wasn't imagining things.

Again the emotions seemed to flood me and I felt very uncomfortable. Where was Ben when I needed him? Well, of course, he was standing right next to me.

He said, "It's tough, I know, Henry. But trust me, it'll pass. Hopefully they'll all get it out at the funeral." I looked at him, at a loss for a reaction. He put his arm around my shoulder.

"Be strong, old friend."

Poor Elaine, I felt terrible for her. She'd been married as long as I'd known her, but I'd often sensed it was a careless and loveless match. After some moments I could agonize no longer and we left.

I say left, but in reality we just reappeared at the secluded park bench. It was as if I'd taken a nap and had a dream. "Wow," I said, "That was worse than dying."

He smiled, "I know, and there's many who'd agree with you. Transition is often absurdly easy, so easy in fact that many refuse to believe they're dead. We try convincing them one way and another, but our efforts often fall short until they're drawn by the grieving relatives."

I shook my head and looked around: The trees and bushes seemed to be glowing.

"Henry, if you're finding all this too much to take in at once, don't feel bad, almost everyone does. Some people just flip out and shut down completely."

"And then what?"

"There are rest homes specifically set aside for them. Two or three days sleep with some color and sound therapy thrown in usually brings them around."

Color and sound therapy, now that sounded mysterious. I asked if I would ever be able to see it in operation. The answer was probably— I might, if I was lucky, be able to get a little taste of it. I said I was intrigued.

We returned to the guest house: Phoebe was behind the desk. I was thrilled to bits. Unfortunately she could not join us for drinks and laughed when I told her how crestfallen I was.

Ben brought over a couple of beers from the bar. Mine tasted marvelous. I surveyed the scene around us: It could have been a hotel lounge almost anywhere in North America. Relaxed people chatted and chuckled. It was incredibly hard to believe they were all dead.

Ben said, "I know, I remember just how it feels. Everybody looks so incredibly alive, you wonder if you're being tricked."

I nodded.

"Trust me, we get quite a few religious types who think just that. They try to ward us off with demon talk. I can't tell you the number of times I've been called a tempter. Get thee behind me and all that."

"So what do you do with them?"

"There's a couple of Christian and Moslem communities nearby, and now that I think of it, Jewish and Hindu as well. I'm sure all the major sects are covered one way or another. We just telepath a message over and a welcoming committee shows up to guide them homeward. Of course they make sure to keep up an angelic front. Darn, they look funny sometimes."

"And they go away with them just like that?"

"Ever seen a good Catholic refuse the parish priest?"

"No, I guess not."

My golfing buddy Jack appeared at this point, slapping me heartily on the shoulder. "How are we doing, Henry? Getting adjusted?"

I had the distinct impression he was trying to provoke me, so I refused to take the bait and informed him that I was doing just fine. He settled himself beside us and made some small talk with Ben, the references of which I just couldn't make out. I had the feeling this was also to irk a reaction out of me.

He turned to me quickly and said, "So, Henry, have you felt the pull yet?"

"Yes, unfortunately. Ten times worse than dying. Lord, if people only knew what it did to you."

Jack laughed heartily. "And I bet you resisted bravely. That good old stiff upper lip holding you in good stead, is it?"

I grinned widely. "I'm not taking the bait, Jack, no matter what you do."

"That's my boy, Henry; never say die, eh? Excuse me while I get a drink and maybe Ben will give you the lowdown on your funeral."

Apparently I had to attend my own funeral. Ben said not to worry, almost everyone did it here, in fact in some spots it was all the rage, with people one-upping each other on attendance figures and flowers. The pull, he went on, was quite irresistible. So many people all thinking of you. Resistance, he claimed, was more or less futile. And besides, it did some people a lot of good. Those in denial. Seeing themselves in a coffin being wept over often worked wonders.

I can tell you quite plainly I was not thrilled at the prospect. The first pull was bad enough. I was quite content in this lovely guest house, thank you. And so I should be, added Jack, sitting down to his drink, it's the best in the neighborhood. I should thank him for bringing me here.

We sat there chatting until someone mentioned dinner. Was I hungry? I had to think about it. Sure, why not. They led me to the dining room. Banquet tables were heaped with goodies, mainly salads, cheeses, bread, and fruit.

Ben said to grab what I wanted and not to feel self-conscious about it. I noticed Jack hardly ate a thing. He said you lost all appetite when you'd been in spirit a few years. It was like a habit that slowly withered away. "Just another satiated desire," he grinned. Ben munched away happily on some exotic-looking salad. He told me he could feel his appetite slowly waning, but that he still enjoyed small indulgences.

What they didn't tell me was that the food quickly disappears when you stop thinking about it. Yes, you taste, chew, and swallow, but no, digestion does not take place and neither does defecation. They didn't tell me because I wasn't ready to hear it. New arrivals rarely are.

Although it took me quite some time to see it, I was being coddled like a baby, which is really what you are, a newborn in a new land. A death there is a birth here, and a birth there is a death here.

At Ben's suggestion we attended a performance at one of the local theatres. Much to my relief Jack begged off, saying he had prior commitments, but he made sure to remind me to enjoy my own funeral and spare no expense. I gritted my teeth and smiled.

From the small-town atmosphere I was expecting a fairly amateur theatrical, but I was pleasantly surprised with a very smooth and effective staging of Noel Coward's *Blithe Spirit*. Its charm and gaiety were just the sort of reprieve I needed from the funeral cloud.

In the lobby afterwards it was just like any posttheatre crowd, bubbly with banter and laughter.

"I know," said Ben, as we moved through the jostle. "It's damn hard to see all these people as dead. You're expecting them to be somber, reflective, and maybe gloomy?"

"You said it."

"Well, to be honest, that does exist too, but not on this level. Perhaps when you're more settled, someone, maybe even me, will take you there. But there are always those like yourself, who adapt quickly and whose natural effervescence quickly rises to the top. It's for types like you that places like this were made."

"And you, where did you land up?"

"Oh, not too far from here, in one sense. I was on the West Coast when I passed over, northern California, but having the heart condition for years I wasn't so shocked and actually quite pleased to be free of my chains. You know, you get really tired of being careful and avoiding any kind of strenuous activity. You get so you secretly crave excitement. Anyway, my thrill at being so suddenly freed was the kind of joyful vibration that you need to be here, although it was the West Coast version of here. Beautiful forests everywhere."

"And if you'd died in Arizona it would have been hot and dry."

"Certainly the landscape would be similar, but not the heat. At this level the temperature is always just right."

And that gave me something to think about when I turned in for the night. Not that it was dark, mind you. It never seemed to get dark here. Ben suggested pulling the curtains if I was having trouble sleeping. I told him I wasn't but that I'd try it anyway.

The intricate weave of the fabric was so beautiful that I stood contemplating it for many minutes before daring to move them. Their heavy textures did not allow for translucence and a cozy dimness settled on the room. I folded my clothes, washed, and turned in, still not sure whether I was entering or leaving a dream.

PART TWO

"THE ENDLESS DAY AFTER"

Seeing a Suicide Grin

I opened my eyes after what I assumed to be the passage of several hours. Well, the room was still there, in all its sedate and reassuring calmness. A quiet suffused the place, with no low level hums or whirrs, the kind I thought reserved for five-star accommodations. Contentedly and delightedly immobile, I gazed at the cream-colored ceiling, wondering what kind of adventures lay in wait for me now. Ben had said he would call again soon, but my time was really my own and he didn't want to interfere. I'd been glad of his company and would be, no doubt, again, but the thrill of a job- and wife-free life consumed any temporary loyalties arising from my transition. Visions of Veronica, Reid, and Elaine all took their little bows, but I quickly applauded them off stage to resume my selfish pleasures. Who knew how long I'd be able to do that.

A leisurely shower followed by an excited lunge towards the dining room would sum up my inner contradictions at that point. An inward calm that seemed to serve as a launch pad for various thrilling possibilities. I hailed two residents in the hall. "Listen, ya gotta tell me, are you dead, too? Hi, I'm Henry, just got here yesterday."

They both laughed. Dale and Marg had been here a couple of weeks and were due to leave anytime. A small house nearby had become vacant and they had applied through the usual channels.

"But hell, Henry, stay here as long as they'll let you," Dale grinned.

"Yes, it's a wonderful spot," continued Marg. "We'd stay if we hadn't found this darling little house. It's just too lovely to turn down."

I enthused about deadness and they agreed: It was certainly the most fun they'd ever had, and they'd been to both Bermuda *and* Cuba before the revolution. We walked down to breakfast, new best friends. I was to visit them as soon as they settled in. I was just going to love it here, Marg insisted, I was to just wait and see. I told her I'd be happy to. The dining room was just as bright and cheerful as the night before. We settled at a table by a large picture window, and with coffee, orange juice, and muffins at the ready, we devoured each other's lives and concerns.

Dale and Marg had been childless for so long their sadness had settled into acceptance, and now that they were here it was just one less thing to fret over. Besides, they both had aging parents whose shock and grief still haunted them.

"They told us it would pass after the funeral, but I guess it's early days yet," Dale offered.

"Oh honey, don't be bothering Henry with all that."

I assured Marg that it was no bother, that everything about this new world fascinated me. And it did, that was no lie. I asked how they died. Dale had drowned on vacation, a sudden storm on a fishing charter, his first one too. Marg had stayed in the hotel with a headache and then took her own life three days after burying Dale.

"I just couldn't see the point of life without him, so I stuck my head in the oven. My church pals sure were surprised, I'll tell ya."

Seeing a suicide grin, that was another first.

Dale grimaced, "My fault really. I was hangin' around Marg like a lost puppy, trippin' her up everywhere she went. Didn't even see my helper for about four days. Guess I won't go fishin' again though."

Dale had been a pharmacist, Marg a beauty consultant, and both had been regulars at different churches.

"Not a good idea in our town, but we did it anyways. Guess we just like to be different, that's all."

Neither had given much thought to the afterlife, just kinda assumed it was there, somewhere in the beyond. Dale had spent more time wondering about all those little guys in flying saucers and where in heck they came from than the afterlife. He still didn't know, and nobody they'd met here so far would clue them in, although Dale was just certain that someone up here must know. Marg wasn't much for all that, although she had to admit there were many planets out there and surely somebody had to live on them. Why would God create them and leave them empty? It just didn't make sense, at least to her. They'd been told there was quite a variety of churches in the neighborhood, and as soon as they got settled in they'd be going to a few.

I let them in on a few of my little secrets and tragedies and we commiserated in classic style, as new friends often do. I concentrated on my parents as I thought the whole Veronica-Reid situation might be a bit too much for them. Dale understood; his dad had always been a bit on the demanding side and certainly wasn't happy with his pharmacist career. A doctor had been more what he'd had in mind, but Dale just didn't have the marks, or the smarts really. Marg added that the whole thing had been kinda funny, as her mother had always dreamed of her marrying a doctor, but the two boys in her town that'd made it to medical school had married girls they'd met there, sending the whole town into a tizzy. Not Marg though: She'd dated one of them in high school and he'd been so full of himself all night she just about dumped her Boston cream pie in his hair. Besides, when she met Dale at her cousin's wedding, she'd fallen for him instantly. Dale laughed and said he put up quite a fight but he was no match for her charms. His mother had been nearly hysterical about him marrying a girl whose big ambition in life was to be some kind of glorified hair dresser, but he knew that Marg had the goods where it mattered.

Returning to the table loaded with scrambled eggs and fresh fruit, I launched into the Veronica story, at least the opening romantic part. Fortunately I was cut short by the arrival of Constance, who appeared to be some kind of afterlife real estate agent and was just as pretty as every other young woman I'd seen here, and who proceeded to lead her excited first-time buyers off to their dream home down in the valley. Dale assured me they'd be back to visit, and Marg kissed me, ever so sweetly, on the cheek. Constance, alas, smiled and shook my hand.

The Phoebe Factor

I was delighting in the incredible flavor of the fresh pineapple they had there when a pleasant voice beside me said, "Henry, how are you today?"

I looked up to see the lovely Phoebe. I was so pleased to see her I acted restrained and polite. Typical damn Yankee.

She joined me at the table, a glass of orange juice already in her hand. I wanted to nibble on her toes and have her drop grapes into my mouth but, ever the gentleman, said nothing.

"Please don't tell me my grandfather came by again. That would spoil everything."

"No, I've never seen him again. Don't worry, he'll only come if you want to see him."

"How do you know?"

"That's the way it works here."

"I so want you to be right."

"Don't worry about it, I am."

If I mention her radiant smile and sparkling eyes, I will likely sound foolish and besotted. Well, the truth is I was. If she'd told me that God was in the next room signing autographs before leaving for Alpha Centauri, I would've believed her. Instead she just asked me what I'd like to do. Without any further consultations with my doubts and anxieties, I blurted "go camping in the mountains."

Why I wanted to quit the most relaxing bedroom in the known universe for a lumpy sojourn on high meadow grass was not immediately clear, but the Phoebe factor likely had something to do with it. Now I see I just wanted to run and hide. Phoebe calmly informed me that my plans would be no problem, but that the pull of my funeral would likely get to me no matter where I went.

"Don't be so glum, Henry; it'll pass like everything else."

"Do I look that bad?"

"You look just fine, but I can sense what you're going through. Haven't you noticed how you can feel things here?"

I was determined not to mention the ducks and merely nodded my head with an "mnnn." I asked where her family was.

"Oh, they're all still on Earth."

"Even your grandparents?"

"Yes, I passed very young, you see. Don't be sorry, I have plenty of friends here and they are more like family than family."

It wasn't until much later that I was to find just how true this was. At that point I merely suppressed my conventional sympathies in favor of Phoebe's obviously greater wisdom.

In what seemed like twenty minutes we were in a camping supply store, stocking up. The guy behind the counter was a typical backwoods hiker type who could barely restrain his enthusiasm. I took his advice and listened to his stories, all the while imagining how quiet it would be in the hills. Phoebe stood to the side, smiling and seeming to know every third person passing by. Her hometown, I guessed. Phil released me to my own devices with a backpack that seemed to defy gravity. We'd just spent an hour jamming it with all the necessities and it still felt like a load of feathers. Everything seemed to roll up real tight and small here.

Outside the store, on a street so quaint you immediately wondered whether there were any investment opportunities left, Phoebe asked if I wanted to take the bus. I said sure. We strolled a couple of blocks. I finally noticed the number of Negroes around. Phoebe said, without any prompting, "Oh, we're totally integrated here." I was immediately suspicious but bit my lip.

I asked about those who would be uncomfortable with that state of affairs. Phoebe assured me that there were plenty of single-race communities for those who desired them. And single-religion communities, for that matter. People were kind of magnetized to the place that would suit them best, and if they later had a change of heart, they could easily pack up and move on. So my golfing buddy Jack would sense what was the right fit for me? Oh yes, Jack was very good at that.

Just then a rather portly black man stopped us to ask the way to the bus station. Phoebe told him he'd just missed it and to follow us as we were going there. He introduced himself as Cyrus and I shook his hand, asking how long he'd been here, as I was a newcomer myself. About four days, he thought. He'd passed while he was praying and was shocked not to find himself in Heaven. Why, he'd woken up in a church down this very block, sleeping in one of the pews. I couldn't help but laugh at his story, but he seemed so crestfallen I immediately regretted it and apologized.

"That's good, Henry, you wouldn't want to offend a good clean-living southern Baptist, now would you?" While these words, one by one, left his lips, he changed, well, from Negroid to Caucasian, and from portly Cyrus to fit-as-a-fiddle Jack. Sort of quickly and slowly at the same time. I tell you, it was weirder than the ducks, and that took some doing. Of course, I felt like a chump as Jack back-slapped the guilty liberal out of me. I turned to Phoebe and asked if he'd done the same to her when she'd arrived. Phoebe said she'd been too little for that kind of treatment. I told her she looked kind of relieved and she chuckled.

33

Jack, of course, had disappeared the second I'd turned to Phoebe, but as we were arriving at a nondescript building that could've been any number of things, the least likely of which would've been a bus station, I opted for bemused compliance. Even if Phoebe were tricking me, I longed to be caught in her web. We sat on a bench and waited. I could smell magnolias but I couldn't see them.

An extremely modern-looking bus appeared out of nowhere, sleek and quiet. The door hummed open and a driver leaned out and called, "You going to the mountains, mister?" He looked lean and bony and very no-nonsense. Pleasing him seemed to be my part in the play. Phoebe urged me to have fun and waved goodbye. I climbed aboard as nervous as if I were twelve instead of . . . how old was I, anyway? I sat by an opened window and smiled. Phoebe called, "Come back soon if you get bored!" I was, of course, bored already and wanted to squirm my way out of the window and into her arms. But being boring old Henry, I just smiled and waved.

Boring Old Henry

The bus moved at a leisurely pace through rolling meadowland, some of it grassy and wild, some of it with cows and sheep. Short stretches of forest seemed to appear and disappear with pleasing regularity. The hills we were headed toward looked more like mountains by the moment. A very odd mixture of cars passed us going in the opposite direction. I wondered if it were some kind of antique rally. Every once in a while we would stop to let people disembark. Two ladies and a boy, two men, three girls, everyone chirpy and cheerful, and everyone carrying a picnic hamper. I began to think I was missing something. Why didn't I have a hamper and Phoebe by my side?

The driver turned and called, "Guess you got her all to yourself now, mister." I looked around: He was right, the bus was mine. I moved closer to him. "Carl's the name, been here a while, always liked driving folks, always wanted to do it for nothing. It's my calling ah guess."

"I'm Henry, only been here two days, still learning the ropes."

"Well, a newborn! And how d' you like it so far?"

"More than I can say. One couldn't ask for better. And such a relief, too."

"Scared up by all them Bible thumpers, were ya?"

I chuckled. "Well not so much them—just my family, my life really; couldn't stand it any more. Best thing I ever did, coming here."

Carl laughed, he knew that one alright. Wife took the kids and ran off with a neighbor while he was on an overnight to Cleveland. God knows where they went. Left him with a rented house and furniture. Quit his job, went to Atlantic City, gambled till he dropped, got himself into a bar fight, and died on the way to the hospital. Now he drives a bus, goes sailing on the big lake, and helps out at the detox clinic.

"I've taken a few to the mountains. Like yourself, they just wanna get away. Couple came back already, some more still there, I guess."

A while later we pulled up at a park entrance. Wooden fences, a gatehouse with nobody in it. A sign telling you to wait here for the bus. I thanked Carl for his camaraderie and stepped off.

"When you've had enough of all that nature, just come down here and wait and I'll come by for you. Oh yeah, almost every day Eleanor comes by on her bike with some cheese and olives and just the best barbequed chicken."

I thanked him for the tip and waved as he drove off. That was one quiet bus, I thought as I sat down on the bench by the empty gatehouse and surveyed my new surroundings. I decided it was designed for those who wanted to feel alone. There was a kind of reassuring desolation to the place. Comfortably ramshackle, with bits of unidentifiably broken things lying about as if they'd been carefully placed by set designers with pens and clipboards.

My God, I was dead. How terribly strange it all was! And yet so familiar. Was camping here going to be just like camping there? Surely not. An immensity of experience rose before me. The foreverness of it all seemed daunting. Was I to go on like this for all eternity? And if so, why? What grand purpose would be served?

I continued to torture myself in this manner for several minutes and then realized it was all pointless and I might as well enjoy myself, here in the bosom of nature. I'd been told several times that there was nothing to be wary of, no storms, no landslides, no predators. Phil had assured me that this was the home of the lion lying down with the lamb and I was bound to see some strange and wonderful sights.

At that moment the very fact of walking, of putting one foot in front of the other, seemed wonderful. Then I had this peculiar urge to stoop and touch my toes. I removed my knapsack and performed the little ritual. My frame seemed to have been remade with some highly malleable rubber that was a huge improvement over bones and joints. I reached up my arms and began to bend over backwards, wondering just how quickly my progress would be halted. But it wasn't and soon I was a perfect n shape, like the acrobat boy-Henry dreamed of being. The memory of both that dream and my father's nickname for me made me want to kick up both feet to complete the maneuver, but I lost my balance and was quickly a laughing heap. The shock and subsequent hilarity boosted me into a fair semblance of merriment and I kinda wished I had someone to share it with.

Instead of moping over that one, I tried bouncing on my feet. A foot, two feet, then three. All quite effortless. Boring old Henry almost didn't recognize himself. How could the Earth be so like a trampoline? No, it's my new rubbery feet.

"Hello!" called a lady's voice. "Hello!"

I turned my head as I bounced and could immediately see a tall slim gal with her hair in a bun and big glasses, standing by an ancient-looking bicycle, waving. Like an idiot I waved back. She seemed pleased with my reaction and I felt emboldened to bounce over towards her. The last time I'd been this giddy I'd fallen and broken my arm, losing three weeks of school in the process.

"My, what fun you're having," she laughed as I arrived by her, still bouncing.

"Have you ever tried it? It's the most amazing fun."

"No, but I might now."

As soon as she said this I stopped and apologized for my eccentric behavior. "I'm not always like this."

"I know, we're all a bit perplexed when we arrive. Don't worry, it'll pass. My name's Eleanor, by the way, and I was wondering if you'd like some cheese and olives for your trip."

"Why thank you, Eleanor, I would indeed. The bus driver said you might be about."

"Yes, I live close by and come cycling by a couple of times a day. It is beautiful country and I just love the breeze in my hair." I ignored the bun and agreed. She reached into the broad wicker basket attached to the handlebars and brought out a neatly wrapped brown paper package. I thanked her profusely. Perhaps I'd also care for some roasted chicken? That, too, soon arrived in my hands.

"Well then, I shall be off now. Do have a lovely time, and don't worry about a thing."

"Thank you, Eleanor, you've been most kind."

She mounted her steed and was off, waving like, well, some old-fashioned gal in an English film.

I walked off in search of some woods, my step still light but my giddiness encased . . . just in case.

I tramped through meadows of long grass and wildflowers, delighting in the birdsong and whispers of breeze. I told myself I had not a care in the world, but something nagged at me—not a care in this world perhaps. Something considerably bigger than a copse loomed on the side of some upcoming hills. I thought, yes, just what I want.

I found a pleasant spot, close enough to a pebbly brook that its chattering would be my constant companion. I'd always had a soft spot for water over rocks and couldn't think why death would change that. What did death change, then? I wondered as I opened up my little tent, and continued to wonder, stretched out on the bank, nibbling at some of Eleanor's goodies. Like everything here, the food tasted incredible. And the water from the stream—ambrosia, straight, no chaser. Amazing. No wonder they called it Heaven. Or did they?

Everything had been so wonderful since my arrival, just like the old books said. How could anyone, me included, ever fear death? Even the ground was soft, you sort of sunk partway into it. No lions or lambs so far, but I had plenty of time. I pulled out the little pillow Phil had suggested and drifted into the most welcome sleep.

Eden and Its Anxieties

Wake up? I don't know, really. I opened my eyes and there were the forest and stream, exactly as they were a moment before. Maybe hours had passed, maybe days. Should I go to town and see if a hundred years had gone by? A vague thrill at the prospect made me shiver. No, I'd stay here and listen to the voices of the brook. I lay there entranced, happy as a clam. You get the picture.

Peacefully afloat in this deciduous eternity, I kept wondering if I should be making some decisions. After all, this was a momentous time in my—well, would you call it life? I suppose. What else would you call it? I mean, it obviously wasn't death, unless death was an intricately intertwined series of elaborate stage productions mounted by an enormous theatre company with bottomless resources. Heck, everything was just too darn real.

I recalled my two Catholic buddies in college, Clarence and Larry, telling me that the spiritualist Heaven I'd been reading about must be some kinda Purgatory because for sure only Catholics were going to Heaven. As far as they were concerned Purgatory was where you shed your excess baggage, like the sins of pride and arrogance and lust. Kinda like losing weight, Clarence liked to say, patting his belly and grinning. Mostly we played poker for pennies and tried to forget the weight of our studies for a few hours. They were good guys, the two of them, cutting through my reticence and general all 'round stuffiness, helping me be a bit more human really, making me marriageable, as Larry liked to joke.

And he wasn't far wrong: After a year or so with them I met Veronica at one of his family get-togethers—a barbeque so big they reserved space in a park and put up cousins from Baltimore for the weekend. She looked so pretty then, so pleasant and charming, I couldn't bear my bachelor isolation another minute and asked her for a date. Like most young men, I didn't realize I was signing my life away with a marriage, but I didn't care to think of that now. Of course, trying not to think about something brought on a whole host of uncomfortable images. A parade of minute embarrassments passed through what I used to call my mind's eye, each one somehow more acute than the last. It culminated with my most recent visit back home and a tussle with my mother. She doubtlessly wanted to comfort me in my born-again bachelorhood, but I could not take to her fussing and meddling and more or less told her to back off. I knew I had hurt her, but I'd felt it was necessary. Her caring had always been contaminated with the urge to control, and with my other boss on vacation I was in no mood for a replacement. I relived the scene now, in all its ragged intensity. There seemed to be no escaping her hurt: It gnawed at me, as relentless as only guilt can be. There was no squirming out of it, as I might have done on Earth; it was to be experienced fully, and as I fell helplessly into it, I began to see its source—the crib death of little Ann, the sister I'd never seen.

Of course, of course, of course! How could I not have known? My mother was terrified of losing me as she'd lost her only girl. And now her worst nightmare had come true. Without any warning I was in her bedroom, watching her writhe and moan on the bed. The visuals were tough enough, but being somehow able to feel the raw edge of her wound as if it were my own was too much. I caved in, collapsed, call it what you will, but not a shred of dignity was left as I wept on the bed beside her. Feeling her almost suicidal sadness felt like the greatest shared intimacy ever between us, and yet I knew she could not feel me as I did her. The sadness was practically unbearable, but try as I might, I could not summon the strength to leave the room. I was compelled to stay and reel in the pain. And as this was the sort of thing I tried to avoid at all costs on Earth, my discomfort level shot through the roof.

Mother felt she had nothing to live for. Father was this emotionally distant support mechanism that she could easily do without, and the brass letter opener on the bureau beckoned. I watched as she bumbled and weaved toward it. What a terrible thing to do on the eve of my son's funeral, I felt her think, but I'm beyond caring what people will say. Life has given me nothing worth hanging on to . . . all that I loved has been taken from me . . . my house, my jewels, all mean nothing.

Something made me grab hold of myself. I stood and tried to put thoughts in her. I said, or thought, really, I'm here with you now, Mother, can't you feel me? She held the letter opener in front of her face and stared at it. I fixed a stare upon her and thought, Don't do it, don't do it, Father needs you. She ran a finger around the tip, trying to guess its possible efficacy. Don't, Mother, I thought: I love you. It was lousy reasoning, but something in her fluttered, moved, I don't know. The fever broke, the swelling subsided, and the letter opener returned to the bureau. Her thought was, Well I'm glad that's over, and she moved purposefully towards . . . what . . . oh, the telephone, and suddenly she was Mrs. Ernest Henry Turner, daughter of American rectitude.

A wave of relief seemed to sweep me from the room and I was back on the soft grassy bank, hearing the babble of water over rocks. In seconds I was so secure in the surroundings of this Eden, my minidrama of moments before was soon fading. But when would the next bout be?

I had not a clue, but the trip from Heaven to Hell and back again definitely had me flabbergasted and would never, I suspected, be used as an ice breaker at cocktail parties. Did they even have cocktail parties here? Well, I'd seen almost everything else, so why not? Dead people do just what they want, Jack had said during my first day dead. Maybe he was right. Maybe it was the land of heart's desires after all.

I wanted to get up and walk, explore, look for birds, but the river's music seemed to stupefy me, hold me hostage in its textures and chimes, so I lay there like some vacationer, too sapped by sun to even slip into the pool. Instead I thought about sister Ann, that dreadful emptiness at the core of my family's bustle and ambition. So deeply buried were the scars, so honored were the suffering and sacrifice, I could see I'd inherited them like some emotional family heirloom. But what to do with them, that was the question. Maybe they'd just fall off, like the excess baggage of Clarence's Purgatory. But somehow I couldn't see it; they were more like baggage to be carried but hidden from view.

Cashews from Heaven

I suddenly remembered a little pamphlet Phoebe had slipped into my bag as I'd walked to the bus. She'd just smiled and slapped my back and I hadn't bothered to look. I fiddled about till I found it. *What to Do Now That You're Here* it was called. Hmmn. On the first page were the words "A Manual for the Duly Impressed." Well, that was me, duly impressed. Duly? I'd say deeply. This place, this world, was so wonderful and amazing, I could only bear to think about it in short bursts. Its magnificence was just too much for my tiny brain. So, duly impressed? Yeah.

Next page said:

If your passage was smooth and your arrival uneventful, you'll probably be settling into the vacation atmosphere without a hitch. Don't worry about it or feel guilty for your leisure. Your loved ones do miss you, but you can always enter their dreams. Those who got here before you enjoyed it just as much, and those who will arrive sometime later will be just as pleased. No one misses the boat for eternal summer. It always has been here and it always will be here. The surroundings may shift to accommodate fashionable expectations, and the staff may move on to other locales, but the enormous relief of our stress-free communities, with their unparalleled beauties and opportunities for praise, will always be required, if not for those arriving from Earth, then for others imported from the all-important elsewhere.

That was intriguing, the all-important elsewhere. I thought of Dale's interest in flying saucers: Maybe dead folk from other planets were here, too. Maybe eternal summer was some kind of solar system collection point, some crossroads in time and space. Entering the dreams of your loved ones; I shuddered at the thought and dismissed it. For others maybe. The idea of eternal summer always being here seemed intriguing, though. Was Heaven a place where nothing ever changes? Or was this Heaven at all? The foothills of Heaven perhaps.

I flipped to the next page.

Eternal summer is not divided on ethnic or religious lines. All are welcome—to be and to stay. Guides brought you here after your transition because they thought you would be comfortable with things as they are. If you find your comfort level dropping then let us know; we can help. Mention your situation to the person who gave you this book. They're all old hands and know the ropes. Relocation is not a problem; there are many other wonderful communities hereabouts who welcome newcomers. Some long for the mountains, others the desert, yet others the open sea. All are available. From the electric charge of cities to the silence of the hermitage and everything in between: We can help you choose. Sports, education, the arts and sciences; hobbies, crafts, religion, and spirituality; entertainment, employment, and community service—all this and more is yours for the asking, so don't be shy.

A guide to the afterlife? A brochure for a holiday resort, more like. Still, it was more like a vacation than anything else so far. I nibbled on a bag of mixed nuts. Wow! Crunchy, meaty, sweet. Better than any cashews ever invented. Cashews from Heaven.

The next page:

Hankering after Hell? Don't be ashamed, lots do. Relief from not ending up there often melts into an insatiable curiosity about what you might be missing. Sign up for one of the guided tours and be ready to be shocked. It's not a pretty picture: tormented, lonely, angry, addicted, sad, ignorant, and stupid. Don't take our word for it; see for yourself and return to your relief. And if compassion compels you, the rescue missions are always looking for fresh recruits.

I folded the pages and lay back to think. I thought of my first day dead. Just yesterday I was driving through forests on winding country roads, relishing my escape from workaday life. A small hill, a tight bend, and I was a statistic. Seconds of regret followed by moments of mystery and wonder. Then something I'll call hovering sadness made wet with tears. Then Jack with all his razzamatazz. Suburban Connecticut. The ducks. Well, that was enough of that.

Like all good Protestants I turned instead to pain and sadness. After all, that was my inheritance, was it not? Sins of the father, salvation through slogging. In seconds I was punishing myself with Veronica and Reid. No sooner said than done, I was with them. Veronica, dressed only in one of Reid's shirts, was standing at his stove making coffee. Reid, I was betting, was still in bed, stroking his beard and luxuriating in his manhood. I was horrified that Veronica would stand so close to a window nearly naked, but Reid had always brought out the fallen woman in her. She'd howled when I'd told her that, during our most recent partner swap. "Henry, you're such a stuffed shirt. Get with it, will you, women don't have to be princesses any more. Why don't you get your little Elaine to loosen up a bit. It would do her the world of good." Little Elaine was indeed only five two, but traveling together on the commuter train did not make her my mistress, a fact Veronica could never accept. She was demure and attentive in an admiring faithful servant kind of way, but it was only now that I could start to see Veronica's repeated assertion, that she was obsessed with me and would follow me anywhere. Firstly, she was married, however unhappily, and secondly she was Catholic, just like that damned papist Kennedy, as father would never let me forget. Veronica promised me that she would howl like a banshee if I ever got her in bed, an odd thing for most wives to say, but not in the slightest for Veronica, especially after a week with Reid, who seemed to stoke a fire that I couldn't even see.

Veronica sauntered into the bedroom, the open shirt swaying about her, carrying two mugs. I just knew they were going to talk about money. My money. They did. I absented myself before anger got the better of me. That escape vacated just enough thought space for Elaine, who was alone in her bedroom, sobbing, a photograph of me in her hand. Her eleven-year-old stood in the doorway, watching for a moment before turning away. He called from what sounded like the kitchen. Elaine shouted, "It's by the front door, honey, just where you left it," and then sat back on her bed, dabbing her cheeks with a hankie. I sat beside her and placed my arm gingerly on her shoulder, eager, for a second, but kinda relieved that she didn't notice. I mean, what would I have done if she did?

Odd sensation, being a ghost. Oh, you can read ghost stories till you drop, but there's only one way of really understanding, and that's to be one. Totally enmeshed but completely absent, there but not there. I remembered how thoughts had affected my mother, so I thought: I'm sorry, Elaine, I kinda took you for granted. I didn't realize how much I meant to you. Part of me thought: You liar, you just didn't want to piss off the old man. You're so strait-laced it's sad. Another part of me disagreed and wanted to mount a sterling defense. Elaine's falling back on the bed to weep some more coincided with a third voice that disagreed with the first two. The combination was deadly and I flew from the room in a flurry of escapist confusions.

I was lying back on the grassy bank, thinking again. Sharp, agitated thoughts, rippling with anxieties and angers, but still easier than actually being there. The jagged intensity of emotions and thoughts, explosions for which I seemed to have no defense whatsoever, exhausted and frightened me. I recalled what I'd been told about funerals—you never miss your own—and cringed.

To divert myself I turned and edged toward the river bank, to dangle my fingers in the trickling water. Like a child I was soothed by the familiar delight, and a gentle playfulness chased the angry shadows. As I gave way to the childish feelings, I seemed to enter the magical world of childhood itself, of which my own was but a small part.

Playing nurse and doctor in kindergarten, Matty's fingers tracing arcs on my thigh, giggles. Running in circles, waving handkerchiefs, and squealing. Watching blue dragonflies close up, waiting for turtles to plop into the river. Matty's seventh birthday party, where Tricia kissed me in the coat closet. Sleepovers at Tom's grandmother's farm, watching the clouds sail past the moon and imagining the lives of the cloud-people. Fluffy fairies who flew to the moon for Thanksgiving. Candy that I couldn't have, no matter what. Falling asleep hanging my head out the bed to see everything upside down and waking up with a sore neck. Learning that hiding things under the mattress was smarter than hiding them under the bed.

Phoebe, Guinevere, and Jack

Somewhere in the middle of all this I actually did sleep. Another refreshing bout of who knows how long, a dreamless vacation from my brain's endless activity. And I still hadn't made it inside the tent. This must be one of those no-rain, no-night, perfect-room-temperature forests, I thought. Must make a note of that and ask someone. Phoebe maybe.

I unwrapped one piece of Eleanor's barbequed chicken and set myself to wandering. The chicken, of course, was out of this world. Did one ever become satiated with such marvelous food? Another question for Phoebe, if I ever saw her again. I soon found an area downstream that was awash in ferns and home to a family of tiny waterfalls. After much delighted exploring I realized that three small streams converged here, collecting in an artfully designed and executed pond, perhaps fifty feet by thirty, whose intricate and delicate banks whooshed me into wonder and then more tears. Wounded by joy, I thought, as I burbled away.

The forest that made you glad to be alive was my final analysis upon returning to the safe ground of dry cheeks. Dead, and glad to be alive: That just about summed it up. And no animals so far. Some kind of museum forest perhaps. Perfect ponds, perfect ferns, perfect trees. Maybe the animals had forests of their own. A lovely chorus of birdsong kept me company from somewhere high up in the leafy boughs, but could I see one of them? Not a chance.

For no particular reason, I moved in the general direction of my campsite. Two figures rose from the ground as I approached, one waving, "Henry!"

Oh my, it was Phoebe and somebody else, somebody even more beautiful than she. I called, "Hello there!" and grinned, disguising, I hoped, my inner panic.

When Phoebe introduced me to Guinevere I held out my hand and announced I was very pleased to meet her. She took my hand and giggled. Much to my embarrassment Phoebe joined in. Phoebe then suddenly hugged me and urged me not to be so serious. I thought, I dunno, I'll do anything for another hug. She said, "I heard that!" and gave me another. Now I started laughing.

The laughter must've loosened me up because I suddenly asked Phoebe's friend why she had such an old-fashioned name. Normally, I'd be all gentlemanly reserved on first meeting. And her answer kept us laughing: "From an old-fashioned picture book." Whereas women I'd known were often charmed by medieval chivalry (Elaine was one), I'd never quite understood the attraction. Those primitive and bloodthirsty times felt quite unredeemed by the legends that romanticized them, at least to me. I much preferred the age of enlightenment, with all its civilized discourse in coffeehouses and at dinner tables, with religion and all its scourges safely back behind church walls.

Phoebe said she wanted to show me a part of the forest she loved. Being fascinated with all things Phoebe, I gave my immediate assent and off the three of us went. We trekked in the opposite direction from which I'd just returned, slightly uphill and into a thickening bush along

Phoebe = Ann

a delightfully winding trail. Finally we plateaued into a clearing, the edge of which overlooked a small valley of rolling meadowland. Perched in the far end of the vale stood the grand villa of some wealthy family, with what looked like all their neighbors' children over for a birthday party. Crowds of the little rascals bobbed and weaved about, as if many butterflies were being chased.

It was indeed a pretty sight, and I said as much to Phoebe. Privately I was glad they were at a distance. I was not in the mood for the kind of racket they'd be making. I followed the women's example and sat to enjoy the view. Was this what Phoebe had wished me to see, I asked. It was. And she was pleased I enjoyed it, for it brought her to something she wished to mention. I froze, a pleasant smile plastered on my lips. A lovely and delightful woman she may be, but I was in no way ready to have children with her. Surely that wasn't how they did things here. Guinevere giggled again. I turned to join in, but a staid embarrassment kept me rooted to some old reliable reticence. It was boring old Henry again, and I wished he'd go away and never come back.

"Henry, dear," she began, "your sister, Ann, the one you never met . . ."

"And how do you know of her?" I asked, failing quite miserably to keep the indignant tone out of my voice.

She went on calmly. "I know because I am she." Her hand touched mine. "I am baby Ann fully grown."

I sat silent for a moment and then began, once again, to weep. Both women consoled me with such a genuine, caring gentleness I wept more instead of less. Doubtless the experience was ultimately to my benefit, making my repressed emotions more accessible, even as I gained a much deeper understanding of my tiny place in the universe, yet twinges of plain old-fashioned shame pull at me even now.

As I had never so much as met sister Ann, it must have been the specter left by her absence that grieved me so. Feeling it pour out of my mother so recently had certainly sensitized me. Phoebe said not to worry, that it had all been for the best, as mother's wounded heart had showered its reservoir of love onto me, making her, yes, overprotective and manipulative, but ensuring that she actually expressed her nurturing nature this time around.

Tears now gone and curiosity reawakened, I queried her phrase "this time around." Phoebe assured me there'd been several others where love of status, power, possessions, and just plain vanity had perverted and ruined her mothering instinct. Was I connected in any way to those times? Yes, Phoebe allowed, but I wasn't to worry about that right now. I asked if it would be too shocking. Maybe, I was told. Guinevere nudged me and said, "I can tell you about one if you like."

"Oh no, you too!"

"Yes, I was your sister once. But we had a sad end. A house fire. Suffocated under our sheets. Off to Heaven together holding hands, so sweet."

I accused her of telling tales. But Phoebe insisted not so. She was our governess back then, and the tragedy made her long for her own children and so she married the young man she'd been resisting and, as she said, "forged a brood." I laughed at that and asked if she'd felt guilt over the fire. Apparently not, as it had been her day off. It all seemed so carefree and silly. Past lives can be like that, Phoebe added sagely, especially when you're clear of all the emotional baggage.

I asked if we might walk some more. My wish was granted. Looking back, it is obvious to me now that my intellectual curiosity over these revelations was being swatted by my emotional inability to cope with them, but at the time I just knew I wanted to walk. Phoebe quietly led the way along meandering single file paths through thick, vision-restricting undergrowth. From time to time we would appear in small clearings and stop to listen to the whispers that surfaced in the apparent silence. Each time, Guinevere would quietly slip her hand in mine. Try as I might, I could not either recall or believe we had perished in some house fire together decades before, but I tried, each time, to return her sweet smile with one of my own.

Finally I uttered a question: Were everyone's first days after death like this? Phoebe said of course not, they were as varied as could be, as varied as people's lives on Earth. Did some folk live in cities as ugly as the ones on Earth? Apparently so; on what she called the lower levels there were virtual replicas of Earth plane cities, where the lost and fearful lived and wandered in mental Hells of their own making. When I got settled and felt up to it, I could sign up for one of the guided tours. Guinevere added that she and Phoebe had perhaps erred in thinking these revelations would help me; she was sorry if they disturbed me unnecessarily. I thanked her for her graciousness and said I probably just needed a few days to think it all over. Besides, didn't I have that funeral to get ready for? Oh yes, Phoebe chuckled, I'd have to get out my best suit for that.

Phoebe then led the way back to my little campsite. It was with a sigh of relief that I watched them go, and a whisper of anxiety as I realized I was being left to my own devices. True to my old self, I coped with ambiguity by eating. Though my appetite seemed small, the food here was so delicious, I savored every mouthful. Like a boy, I lay on my belly, flat out over the stream and cupped my hands for water. The taste was out of this world. Mountain stream refreshing times ten. Then I lay back to nap. Was it an avoidance nap, or just a nap nap? I didn't know and couldn't really summon up the energy to care. But I did disappear into the contentious issue we call sleep.

From there I emerged into a very three dimensional drama of a church service in progress. Some of the faces looked very familiar: a few of my father's business associates, several of my mother's lady friends, two aunts I hadn't seen in a decade, a handful of cousins and nephews. Once again I merged with my mother's crying, her sobs convulsing me, and when I freed myself from that, I got sucked into Elaine and her vortex of grief. Her sadness and unrequited love mixed with my selfish reticence and guilt. What a bastard I'd been! I could've taken her out to dinner, we might have dated on the sly, it would have made her supremely happy. But no, I had to do the right thing, the upstanding citizen of the suburbs burdened with a sex-crazed wife. It had been the psychiatrist or the stiff upper lip, and like the discretion slave I was, I'd gone for the lip as the path of least resistance and maximum camouflage.

My appearance in her aura seemed to instantly magnify her grief, and a thought quickly occurred to me: If I was to be any help at all, I would have to free myself from her immediate vicinity. I yanked myself out, as it were, and attempted some soothing messages of apology and sympathy. In seconds, it seemed, she calmed herself and turned to give a weak smile to the lady friend beside her, a face I vaguely recognized. A friend of my father's got up to give a eulogy. Right, I remembered him now: president of the local chamber of commerce, pillar of the church, and a pompous blowhard who was always trying to get Dad into his failing golf club. And my father, proud and erect, never giving an inch, never flinching as my mother sobbed onto her sister's shoulder, a statue surrounded by pitying admirers. His thoughts were of annoyance and disgust: How could I be so stupid as to let that worthless slut of a wife drive me to suicide? How could I dare embarrass him so? And where was Veronica, missing her own husband's funeral?

There was more to bankers than boardrooms and annual reports. He'd met a few shifty-eyed types at Eugene's club. That plumbing contractor and his pal the automobile parts distributor, they'd have connections. I wanted to shout *It was all an accident!* but as usual he looked like he had his mind made up, so I hovered at the back of the church and watched the rest from a distance. There was an odd-looking fellow by the door that no one seemed to notice but me. He grinned and nodded. I nodded back, wondering how he could see me, Mr. Invisible at his own funeral. Maybe he had died too and had wandered into the wrong church. I went over to inform him of his mistake. Despite all the tension and discomfort, it was still my funeral, and somehow uninvited strangers seemed an intrusion.

As I spoke in hushed tones, suggesting that he might have gotten the wrong address, he changed his appearance, from that of a dignified gentleman dressed immaculately in a dark suit to Jack, my golfing guide who'd rescued me from the collision site just a few whatevers before. As his ruse dawned upon my reprimanding self, I let go with a chuckle and shoulder slap. He grinned in delight, as if to say "fooled another one!" Then he asked if I wanted to see what had happened to Veronica. Feigning disinterest I said, "Sure." He took me by the hand and we disappeared from the church. A second later, a second in which nothing seemed to happen, we were standing on a busy corner of my hometown, looking at an accident scene. A motorcycle had collided with a delivery truck. A knot of people surrounded the scene, presumably taking care of the victims. Jack took my hand and we floated up several feet. Now I could see Veronica and Reid under blankets, people's jackets and sweaters folded under their heads, the delivery truck driver standing there shaking his head. I guessed that Reid had run a red light, as was his habit, a habit Veronica seemed to take undue pleasure in, among others.

Jack whispered, "That was hours ago. Now let's move to the present." Again a second's blankness followed by the appearance of a hospital room. In the beds we stood beside lay, bandaged and sleeping, my wife and her lover. Calmly I turned to my guide and asked if they would survive. "Yes, of course. You didn't think it was going to be that easy, did you? This is just to show you they tried."

"So I don't go around fretting about it, I suppose?"

"Yes, you've got more important things to do."

"Such as?"

"You really want to know? I wouldn't want to spoil your camping trip, after all." Jack had the ability to make me feel like some Boy Scout caught masturbating. Something in me refused to let him gain the upper hand, so I uttered the words that have set my path here in spirit, set it as surely as if I'd said, "Get thee behind me Satan" or, "Give it a rest, you pompous old humbug." The words were "Show me."

Jack grinned again. "I didn't remember you being from Missouri."

I did not have time to react. He grabbed my hand and we suddenly were in a slummy section of a city I didn't recognize. It could've been the wrong side of the tracks anywhere. A bedraggled old tramp was slumped in front of a shack sleeping, an empty bottle in his hand. I waited for Jack to explain. Instead, he muttered, "Any questions?" I enquired as to our purpose. The tramp apparently had died in his sleep but did not know it. And as he'd been virtually friendless, he had not noticed that no one was speaking to him. Another tramp had found his shack—basically a garden shed hidden at the back of an abandoned estate still waiting to be redeveloped—but he'd scared him away by banging on the walls at night. "Typical ghost tactics," Jack assured me, "as old as the hills. Funny part is, they mostly don't know they're ghosts. Too busy being angry at the intrusion."

Jack had been coming by every once in a while to chat with the guy. I asked if he made a point of looking different every time. He grinned and winked. Then he grabbed my hand and we disappeared again. It looked institutional right away. A hospital, a college, an administrative wing of something. High quality paneling and fixtures. The sort of refinement that rose above the smell of disinfectant. I was still getting my bearings when Jack nodded towards a door on our right. A gentleman who could easily have passed for the dean of my old alma mater emerged, carefully closed the door behind him, and shuffled off down the corridor. Jack asked for my opinion. My opinion on what, I queried. What to do. What to do where, I wanted to know. I was, as you might have guessed, completely baffled.

"With the old geezer," he said. "What about him?"

"Well, what about him?" I quizzed.

"He's dead, you dope. Can't you tell?"

Well, as a matter of fact, I couldn't. What were the giveaway signs? Jack motioned me to follow. Down some stairs and out the door. Into a beautifully treed parking lot. Our man looked befuddled and rummaged through his pockets. Finding his keys, he marched toward the only car to be seen. He fumbled with the keys for a moment and then, suddenly nimble, slipped in. Jack suddenly leapt over to the car, seating himself cross-legged right in front of the windshield. And I mean leapt, superman style. He stared in at the occupant and grimaced like a fool. I was so stunned by the leap I forgot to chuckle, but I would've if I'd had the presence of mind.

The car backed up out of its spot and began to drive away. As it passed me Jack hopped off the hood and landed beside me. "Impressed?" he asked. "There's more where that came from."

"I'll bet there is. But what exactly were you trying to achieve?"

"I was trying to get his attention. There's two things you have to understand with ghosts. It's hard to get their attention, and when you do, it's even harder to get them to believe you."

"You had no trouble getting my attention the other day."

"Well, you're a special case."

"How so?"

"Two ways: Subconsciously you met up with me several times during your so-called life as Henry—never, of course, recalling our visits—and consciously you read those books in college that spoke of the life to come, so you had a vague notion that something like afterlife and spirit guides existed, whereas many people don't. The skeptical materialism of the scientific outlook has ensured that modern man only believes what can be proved, and the obsessive physical-plane focus of this matter-conquering phase in our evolution ensures that even when it has been proved, the evidence is ignored or passed over in favor of religious piety."

I must've looked puzzled, for Jack added, "Perhaps you'd like me to repeat that, huh?"

I was chuckling when he grabbed my forearm and we disappeared, immediately reappearing on a barren, windswept hillside overlooking a rocky plain dotted with what appeared to be tumbledown shacks. Jack turned to me and asked if I could guess our location.

"I have a strong feeling that Arizona is not the right answer."

"Correct. One of the many purgatories catering to the wide variety of self-inflicted punishments. And not completely inhabited by Catholics, I might add."

Suddenly we were very close to one of the shacks. Through a window I could see a man in priestly vestments, kneeling and praying. Praying for forgiveness, I thought. "Spot on," said Jack's voice in my ear. "Now watch this."

Without warning Jack's clothing became tattered and old fashioned, his hair gray and wispy, his chin stubbly. A tin plate with a hunk of old bread and a mug of water were held in his right hand. He knocked and walked in. Through the window I saw him leave the plate on a rough-hewn table and leave without a word. The priest did not stir. I had the feeling that he felt himself beneath contempt. Jack, back in his golfer's duds, stood beside me and agreed. I must say, it was nice to be right about something.

I asked about all this rapid change of clothing he seemed so adept at. He told me we'd get to that later. Now he wanted to show me some of the results of the priest's actions. I was intrigued. We moved, or I thought we moved, to a messy bedroom. A teenage boy was lying under the sheets and seemed both agitated and apathetic. I was slightly embarrassed for him and didn't know why.

"Can you tell?" Jack wanted to know.

I wanted to know but I only guessed, and was wrong. He was dead, a suicide from depression. "Altar boy sex a decade ago," announced Jack, as if reading from a list. I was shocked.

"You mean the priest?"

"I mean the priest, and this boy wasn't the only one. The others are still physical, but wounded." By wounded he meant boozing and beating their wives, and by physical he meant still alive. The boy on the bed was dead, but he sure didn't look like it to me. Apparently he just didn't know he was dead, and that made all the difference. He slept after slicing his wrists, slept for weeks, Earth time, convinced that there was no eternal life for suicides, and then woke up into a thought-form replica of his old bedroom.

Jack took me by the wrist and told me to watch as we moved back. It felt like floating, and soon we were about fifty yards away. The bedroom seemed like a bubble surrounded by a grayish haze, a little dream world with no connection to anything except itself. I felt terribly sorry for the child twitching in his ignorance. "That's good," Jack said. "Sympathy is what energizes you in this line of work, and universal sympathy is the best of the lot."

"I take it I have no privacy whatever, then?"

"Not when I'm around, you don't," smiled Jack, all too smugly. "But I do have your best interests at heart, of that you can be sure."

While still grinning at the irony of that, he grabbed my forearm and the scene before me melted into darkness. But only for a second. We emerged onto a beautiful beach—the white sand of a tropical island; the palm trees behind us; the great breakers of a blue, blue sea in front; surfers elegantly riding the crests in a variety of breathtaking stunts. I saw one guy do a somersault right there on his surfboard. To our left was a small group relaxing and joking around. Tanned, handsome, and happy, they seemed the very epitome of healthy human fun, the kind of carefree living most folks just dream about. Some of the men had long curly hair, and some of the women were bare breasted. Some variety of nudist camp, thought I.

"They call it the beach of endless fun," Jack nudged me to look at a sign down a ways. Even though it was about one hundred yards away, I could see the letters quite clearly. Sure enough, it said Beach of Endless Fun.

"Let me guess, Jack: They're all dead and loving every minute of it."

"In a word, yes. But what you don't know is that this is about ten years in the future, Earth time that is. About 1972, or at least a version of it. In your time, the time you just left, these people are still in grade school. Rebelling against consumer society is the farthest thing from their minds."

"I refuse to be shocked. . . ."

"Good start."

"But I want to know how they all got here."

Jack shrugged. "Some are drug overdoses, some are car accidents, some suicides, a couple cancer. What they all have in common is that they came here on holiday and never forgot it."

"This is the Earth then?"

"No, it's the astral all right. Lots of the afterlife is almost identical to its Earthly counterpart. And when pleasure seekers find that they can grow back into their most perfect stage of physical form, they feel like their prayers have been answered. This is the land of heart's desire, of course."

"Is this a surfer's Heaven then?"

"Yes, and yes again. There is a golfer's Heaven, a hiker's Heaven, a pool player's Heaven, and of course, all the religious ones."

At that point one of the bronzed young gods approached, raising a hand in greeting.

"Jack, the man, the golfin' man. How you doin'?"

Jack shook his hand and introduced me as "Henry from 1963."

"Hello, I'm just newly dead, still learning the ropes."

"Well, I didn't think you was from Vietnam. Jack's been bringin' us those damn soldier boys but don't none o' them look like you."

I laughed and wondered why he was imitating a Negro. Jack teased him about some issue I couldn't quite follow. Feeling suddenly brave I asked him why he didn't have a name. His answer stunned me.

"'Cause I ain't nobody. Ah'm free. This is the brotherhood of eternal fun. We's all free."

"And no one's got a name?"

"That's right. We're all free, free as the breeze. No country, no government, no po-leese. And this dude here keeps trying to get me to go to his Heaven. Man, we got Heaven right here. We don't need no God, no Jesus, no church—we're it, and we're it now. Henry, after you get done with Jack and all his magic travelin' show, you come back here and we'll show you some real fun."

I promised to keep his kind offer in mind. Just then, two of the lovely near-naked women appeared beside him, squealed with what I took to be irrepressible joy, and jumped forward to hug me. Their intention was unmistakable and my embarrassment more than likely obvious, but with big smiles they kissed my cheek and were off down the sand, jumping and whooping like teenagers away from their parents. Our friend with no name waved and walked away. Jack touched my hand and we were gone.

We were standing outside a church on a sunny Sunday morning, watching the faithful file in. Organ music filtered out from within. Heads were bowed and voices were low. All the ladies wore hats. We could have been in any of a number of New England small towns. Jack whispered that this was actually not far from the reception hotel I'd stayed at. I asked why no one seemed to notice us. Jack said he had put a protective shield around us, so we might observe unhindered. I steered clear of the "protective shield." I was, however, bold enough to ask whether we were back in my time again. Apparently we were, sort of. These folks were all dead, most of them fairly recently, but some as far back as the thirties and twenties.

A contented crew, Jack mused, somewhat sardonically I thought. I also had a hunch that he'd taken it upon himself to sow a few seeds of discontent among them. Maybe he'd show me his technique. For a time we merely stood at the back and observed. "Decorous piety as befits the smugly assured," whispered Jack. I thought that a little harsh, but who was I to know? Jack had me notice that they were all white, no blacks or Orientals. I took notice as I was instructed. The church atmosphere reminded me of my own funeral service, but a tight squeeze on my wrist jolted me back from that temptation.

Later we stood outside, protective shield removed. Jack was obviously no stranger here. As the congregation mingled after service, some sipping lemonade and nibbling on cookies, several men moved over to say hello and be introduced. I was welcomed warmly by all, pretty much as I would've been on Earth, had I just arrived in town. At least two ladies invited me over for tea whenever I got settled. There was a tennis tournament coming up. And a dance in the community hall. I was welcome to it all. I responded as graciously as my puzzlement would permit. I think

I was waiting for Jack to drop the big one. It was as if people were hoping to smother Jack's tendency to disturb with waves of kindness and sincerity.

The pastor appeared, shaking Jack's hand and then mine. He insisted on being called Teddy. After a few jocularities with Jack he turned to me and said he hoped I wasn't being led astray by Jack's unwarranted ecumenism. I laughed and said that I hadn't noticed any sneaking up on me yet, but if I did I would be sure to waylay it before it did any harm. As someone who had just recovered from the shock of his own funeral, I was gratified that Teddy found this quite funny. He went on to assure me that they were all brothers in Christ there, and any Baptist, Catholic, Lutheran, or Jew was welcome to join in worship. I guessed that Jack had tried to introduce some Hindus and Moslems and had been forcefully refused, but nothing further was said on the matter. Teddy told me to just take my time, that I was in the right place now and there was never any need to hurry. I thanked him for his kindness and turned to Jack, sensing a farewell in the offing. He laughed and, slapping Teddy playfully on the shoulder, threatened to return for the mixed doubles in the tournament. Teddy chuckled, somewhat nervously I thought.

We were allowed to drift off unimpeded. Around a bend in the leafy laneway, my wrist was grabbed and we disappeared. On a city street, somewhere on the wrong side of town, we sheltered from the rain under an awning. Jack stood quietly, as if expecting my question. Which was, how did we manage to travel instantaneously? Jack replied, "That's easy; I know how to do it and I enforce my will upon yours. If you were to resist, it would be much more difficult, but as your curiosity far outweighs any residual belief system, it's a breeze. Besides we've done this already while you were sleeping, so really I'm just reminding you."

I told him I'd take that on trust. He said that was fine. He'd had others who'd accused him of being a demon showing off his powers. But I was ready for it, he was sure. So I was an apprentice of sorts then? "Of sorts," he smiled. He then led me to an apartment on a respectable-looking street, up the steps and through the door. And I mean through. He grinned at my shock. "We're ghosts, can't you tell?" Inside we found three men busy with some kind of preparations. A white powder was being removed from a canister and wrapped into small square paper packets. It had to be heroin. A half a dozen others stood around watching. Watching? Fixated more like. Like gamblers ogling the gaming table. Two of the men by the table scooped up the little packets into leather pouches and made ready to leave. The third moved to an armchair and opened up a paper. The onlookers followed the first two out the door. Jack signaled to me and we followed them. The onlookers had a harried, anxious look about them as they followed the two with the pouches. Jack whispered that they'd split up in a minute and that I was to follow him. Our group went to the right; the others followed their man down a set of steps to a subway station. Our man slipped into a late-model car. I never took much notice of automobiles, but this was a fairly new one.

We all seemed to follow him in, Jack and I in the back, like judges with clipboards, and the other three in the front, eager and expectant in a way I would soon learn that only ghouls can be. Leaning over the driver like ravenous raptors ready to devour anything that moved, they squirmed over who could get the closest. I whispered to Jack, "This is gruesome." He nodded, as if to say "better get used to it." We arrived somewhere after a few blocks and parked. The driver exited in the usual fashion and the rest of us sort of popped through the shell of the vehicle like cartoon characters. This walking through walls and doors stuff was getting to be fun. We all crowded into an elevator and went up to the third floor. Jack and I were so close to the dead junkies crowding the drug courier I couldn't believe they couldn't see us. It was quite a classy apartment building, not the sort of place I expected addicts to dwell in. A refined-looking lady of maybe fifty answered her door, taking two or three packages very quickly and giving the courier an envelope. He returned without hesitation to the elevator with two of the ghouls following. The third had slipped into the apartment during the transaction. I stood with Jack in the hallway wondering what was next.

He asked if I had any qualms about entering the apartment. I answered with a terse pronouncement about how respecting others' privacy was one of the unwritten rules of civilized society, but something told me these circumstances were what they call extenuating. Jack insisted there was an important lesson for me inside, and that if I could set aside my high moral ground for a moment, much could be gained for later use. I acquiesced and we entered. Inside we found the lady making preparations and the ghoul close by gazing intently. In a few seconds she was injecting a solution between her toes. She tensed for a moment and then, sighing, lay back on the couch, enraptured.

Jack leant close and whispered, "Watch closely." I did. The lady slipped further into something like sleep, and the syringe fell from her drooping hand onto the carpet. As the seconds passed in gloomy silence I watched in amazement as a vapory form rose from the prone body. A horizontal mirage mostly like herself floated before us, maybe a foot above her physical form. The ghoul took sudden action, sweeping himself into her body in a flash.

"There you have it my friend, two junkies sharing the same body."

"Is there nothing we can do?"

"No, nothing really until the boredom with the ever-repeated behavior pattern sets in, which could take years. But don't worry, the dead one will get bored when the high wears off and the lady will slip back in. And in that peculiar way the universe has, everyone in the drama more or less gets what they want, at least for the present. Despite all the ugliness of the race, desire has a way of accommodating all comers. And we've got all the time in the world to deliver them from temptation, as the Christians say. And on that note, I suppose you'd like to get back to your camping trip."

"Will this all seem like a dream?"

He grabbed my wrist and we returned in a second. My grassy bank, my birdsong, my musical brook: It was as if I'd never been away. I inhaled it all.

Jack gave me one of his manly goodbyes, telling me not to sweat about any of it, that they were all just dreams, and that my dream of Heaven was just as valid as anyone's. I wondered what he meant when he said "valid" but shook his hand instead. I told him I didn't know whether to thank him or threaten him with a civil suit for ruining my vacation; he said it was all one to him. He'd be just as happy to see me in court as anywhere else. We shared a laugh and he was gone.

I lay down to rest and ponder my dream of Heaven. My pondering lasted the rest of my camping trip and well into what we usually think of as the future. My days as a neophyte were soon to be over, as that dream melted into the greater one of traveler and guide. But as my adventures increased in subtlety and complexity, I could never quite shake the notion that all I was doing was moving from dream to dream.

PART THREE

THE VOICE OF EXPERIENCE

Reid and Me

And to be quite honest, despite an interlude of what would be considered on Earth about two generations and a set of learning experiences as profound and entertaining as they come, I cannot honestly say with any more clarity whether I am entering or leaving a dream, for ease in these worlds is measured by one's ability to shift from circumstance to circumstance with nary a flutter of indecision.

[And the resulting movement leads one to see that change is the only constant, and the consensus realities we call communities are, however beautiful and useful, but temporary resting stops for souls in transit.]

I am one of those souls in transit and my pastime at the moment is part guide, part travel agent. I've had enough of incarnation for now, and maybe forever, despite, I might add, some very tempting offers down there in the physical.

And for the remainder of this text I shall attempt to illuminate both the scope of my activities and the scores of personality types and belief systems

I encounter on my travels, because on those mighty amusing tours of duty I can tune into many people's thoughts, and quite frankly, sometimes it seems as if almost everyone back on Earth wants to know about the after-life. Everyone. Not merely the religious, the philosophical, the idle, and the parents of suddenly dead children, but even confirmed materialists taking time out from a busy schedule of mergers and acquisitions, and scoffing atheists in some of their more quietly anxious moments. So since I'm living here now, your basic semipermanent resident, I might as well devote a portion of my efforts to telling you all about it. Well, maybe not all about it, that's perhaps just a bit too ambitious, but hopefully it will be enough to show up the opulent activity of these resplendent realms.

And since the there-and-back elevator between the physical and astral spheres, now known as the near-death experience, is such a popular topic on TV chat shows, I might as well begin with an example of one of the one-way-only, no-refund specials.

The guy I'm thinking of had just bought it on a motorbike, nothing unusual about that, as common an exit as they come, in fact, but since I was intimately (and karmically) connected with him, I'd had a tip and was there waiting. I'd relieved his regular guardian, who took the opportunity to attend to another of his charges, someone he was quite concerned about, a mother who had just lost a teenage daughter to meningitis and was on the verge of suicide. As an old hand he knew I could take care of an accident scene with ease. Those are the easy ones, really. Bang, straight up out of the body, no fuss, all the muss back there on the ground.

And this case was more or less as expected: a speeding motorcyclist with a devil-may-care attitude, a sudden summer shower, and an over-loaded pickup with balding tires and too much weight in the back. The woman in the pickup was shaken but unharmed, probably stuck between relief and guilt as she pulled out her cell phone. But I had no time for that; my charge was hovering beside me, staring down the thirty feet to the aforementioned muss. I moved in closer.

"So now do you believe in an afterlife, Reid?"

He chuckled and shook his head, a bit embarrassed, a bit amazed.

I had my arm around his shoulder just as I had years before, in our drinking buddy days, before Veronica came on stage and our characters polarized into Mr. Dashing Adventurer and Mr. Conventionally Boring. I led him away from the scene of the crash. Floating, of course. Dead people always do that, don't you know. The bike, a beautiful new BMW just moments before, was nothing he needed to look at now. God only knows how much dough he'd spent on it.

Prizing him away from his pride and joy was easier than I'd expected. Perhaps because he recognized my voice, I'm not sure, but I was able to penetrate the gloom of his grief with remarkable ease. It certainly wasn't the clown outfit, which barely registered on his radar. Maybe it was some kind of leak through from all the times I'd tried to get him to talk about the afterlife when we'd been on Earth together. It was after I'd read those books in college, and even though I'd remained unconvinced, I thought to try and badger him into belief. But he'd always been skeptical, sometimes mocking me as a fanatic or obsessive, sometimes just telling me to shut the fuck up.

But now I was grateful that one of those undernourished seeds had sprouted, for sometimes it can take ages and you have to call for reinforcements, usually Earth-side OBEs, as they seem to have just the right type of energy for the task.

I moved him through the levels quickly and we settled on the lawn of the nearest rest home, where I sat him down and waited with a grin.

"Damn, am I really dead?"

"No, it's just an ugly dream. You'll wake up soon with a hangover and cuss your way to the kitchen for coffee."

"And you'll be just a vague memory, right?"

"Yup."

"Promise?"

"Sure, anything for you Reid, you know that."

It was great to be sparring with him again. It reminded me of the old days, before all those clouds had come between us and made us sensible civilized adults, with consciences to consider and scores to settle.

But rather than drift into all that, which we could easily get back to later, I thought to play into his dream fantasy, suggesting that if he wanted to wake up from a dream, he'd have to sleep first. I nodded in the direction of the travelers lodge. Employing the form of a funky upscale roadside diner, with pool tables, scraggy tennis courts and mini-golf quite beyond repair, it was very useful in settling those of a certain disdainful attitude traveling far from home. He seemed amenable to the suggestion and stood without assistance. I set the pace of a stroll, thinking that would make him the most comfortable. In our heyday we always strolled; it was our shrug to the world.

He seemed no more amazed by the soothing atmosphere of the rest home than anything else. I settled him in a ground floor room with a pleasing view of the meadows leading down and stretching out to low craggy hills.

He admired the view and bounced on the bed. I couldn't help but smile at his happy tourist act. I could see he couldn't bring himself to believe anything, he was just humoring me, praying that I was merely a figment of his imagination, and that by following my instructions he could, by closing his eyes, make all this pleasantness disappear.

I wouldn't call it a standard reaction, but it's far from being unusual. And this position is like any other, on either side of the Earth-bound axis. The more experience one accumulates, the smoother is one's response to any situation that may develop. Many of my temporary charges had passed through this and similar guest houses, only this time the soul was one of my old, perhaps ancient, partners. My usual serene professionalism was challenged.

A circus of conflicting emotions could have derailed us, but I assured him I would be gone when he awakened and left him to lie back when and where he wished.

I had a few words with one of the resident assistants, who made a note of the new arrival and promised to send a message if I was needed. As I was not on any kind of active duty, only on a personal errand, as it were, I thought to whisk back to my own place.

Sometimes I walk, or float gently above the ground, it all depends on one's mood and the circumstances, but at that moment I wanted to return to base and recharge, so I whisked.

Base was now a picture-postcard, English-style cottage, a little larger and less damp than the Earth-plane version, something I'd suffered in on more than one occasion, set in what I pride myself as being a rather chaotic-looking garden, complete with melodious tinkling brook and backyard full of birds. Something of an astral plane cliché, I know, but there you are, I'd always wanted one on Earth and never seemed to quite manage it, what with that rigorous overlay of conventionality.

In my time I've had castles, sheds, and all the shades in between. You might think the infuriating and endless decay of the physical plane would drive me to create something fairly sumptuous, but I refrained, sticking with cozy-as-all-get-out. A hodgepodge of personalized features that seem to fit no one's idea of interior design except mine: terracotta tiles, cherry and oak wood paneling, furniture that you just want to curl around. Prints of all my favorite paintings—Bosch, Vermeer, Turner, Ernst, Duchamp, Monet, Cézanne. One of those hand-painted, dual-manual harpsichords that I can barely play, but what the heck, I'm learning.

I settled in what would pass for a den and stretched out to contemplate the history of my relationship with Reid. I knew I needed to and I knew it would help him. As you know, I'd been dead for some years Earth-time but hadn't really confronted all the issues between us. There had been plenty of others passing through who needed assistance, friends and strangers alike, and basically I just hadn't got around to it. Just like the old Earth-bound excuse, really, too busy to get around to it, sorry. What about Veronica, you're asking. Well, we'll get to that later.

A Typically Twisted Tale

A typically twisted tale, really, the kind that melodramas are made of, the kind you see on TV almost any night of the week. Which incarnation would you like to start with, I say to myself, smirking. I've checked out several of my own for various karmic strands, but not with specific reference to Reid. I could go to the karmic reference center in the city, that will have all the details, including more than a few you'd prefer to forget, but I want to see how much I can summon under my own steam, at least for starters.

So I slowly sink into the appropriate level of consciousness and let the images come. The feeling is quite similar to meditation, at least as I practiced it last time around (I was one of those three-week Zen Buddhists). It's like moving very slowly under warm oily water that is not just full of information, but somehow made of the stuff. I don't know how well that conveys it, but it's the best I can do for now.

Oh, there we are, little brothers playing. What's that? Hay. Right, a barn somewhere. I wonder when. There's a kind of recklessness that suggests Mummy doesn't know and would not approve if she found out. We're rolling around, laughing, but it's a test of strength. He's bigger than me, so I work harder. He's holding me at arm's length, sort of mocking. I shove and he's gone. Whoops, over the edge. I peer down. Of course he has to land on the most skittish horse and get trampled, thereby ruining the rest of my life. He's out of body so fast he doesn't know it; I see his astral form mocking me as if nothing had happened. It's like he's still winning. Bastard.

The rest you can imagine. Mother grieving forever, father deprived of a good hand on the farm. Our younger sister dies of a fever the next year, and then they've only got me to harass, which they do unremittingly. I run away at fifteen and find an army. There's always one around. There's some kind of war somewhere that we're off to. I let the male camaraderie convince me I belong and I bellow with the best of them.

At one point I fully enter the boy's excitement. Up to then it had been a movie, and for the first time he feels really alive—he's on the edge of an adventure and a serving girl smiles at him. Suddenly he has the courage to steal a kiss.

The excitement generated is unbearable; he lies awake all night thinking about her. In the morning they're off and the girl's on the dock, waving. He tries to look manly. I have a hunch they're going from England to France and heading for the Holy Land, but when? That night there's a storm and his ship goes down. His landlubber's terror is quickly ended with a lungful of salty water and soon he's floating above it all in awe.

And that's where Reid meets me, laughing. That is, Reid as he was then. And that's where the memory fades, or seems to. The two figures disappear into a mistiness, and I'm left looking at it. Of course, that's not all. Never is. You have one life with someone, you have several.

Out of the same mist appear two men on horseback. Galloping furies, they're racing from something and sharing great gales of laughter. I pick up thoughts about an invading army whose progress they've cleverly sabotaged. I sense a bridge in a narrow valley burning. Miles away, through winding rocky trails, is a village with wives and children. At the celebration everyone seems to be a cousin or an in-law. There's a feeling of being brigands, or rebels to some oppressive central authority. Allah is evoked and obviously revered. I wonder if they're Kurds or maybe Afghanis. After Allah, tribal loyalty prevails.

Another scene emerges, years later perhaps: A fever has hit the village, decimating it, the women particularly. Reid and I both lose our wives. Great grief ensues. After about a year it becomes obvious the young men have almost no choice. We go off in a wife-hunting expedition. It is something of a success and we return, after much delicate negotiations with suspicious and conniving elders, with several young women from a neighboring tribe (neighboring being only a hundred or so miles), where the recent visit of an imperial army and its persuasive recruiters have left them embarrassingly short of young men.

Unfortunately, Reid and I fall in love with the same girl, and although she marries him and has his children, she and I share a life-long fascination, both learning to read from some kind of wandering scholar, while Reid remains the fearless hunter and provider. The tension is made worse when my wife dies in childbirth and my two-year-old cleaves naturally to his wife, who, not surprisingly, being one of Veronica's forerunners, has one of mine a year or so down the road.

I take to reading in a big way and spend a lot of time in my own tent studying. The tribe seems to recognize the shared-wife scenario, and life goes on through the seasons, with me as the tribal storyteller/priest figure and Reid as the reliable bringer home of the bacon.

Always the daredevil, on one expedition he gets separated from the others and, taking on more than he can chew, gets trampled and gored. It is not a pretty sight and I wonder why I'm looking at it. But not for long, for suddenly I get a call. Telepathic of course: They almost all are up here. I quickly surface from my meditative state and prepare to respond. Instead of a voice sounding in my ear, as it would in your world, a picture forms in my mind.

Being "on call" here is, if anything, worse than down there. On Earth you've still got pagers and phones to distance you. Here it's almost instantaneous. Your friends and colleagues know your wavelength and will not hesitate to use it. The incarnates in your care do not consciously know it, but you are tuned into theirs and have long since learned to distinguish a distress signal from, say, one of delight or perplexity, rather like a mother waking to a baby's murmurs of discomfort.

On Call

This time it's one of my depressed charges, and it looks as though she's gonna slash her wrists in the bath. I whip down there pronto and am standing behind her as she chews morosely on her breakfast toast. She thinks of her husband's betrayal and then of her son's death. The husband she could have handled, he was never one to be trusted and she had found him out on his affairs before, but her son—he was everything to her, her life really, although she didn't know it till he died.

I see if I can influence her thoughts by first suggesting some marmalade for the toast. Innocuous? Hey, I'm acting locally as I think globally. She pushes her chair back and somewhat robotically moves to the cupboard for the jar. I'm surprised: She seemed too focused on the act. Hmm, maybe I can talk her out of it. She seems as if she's going to move through her morning tasks and then, ever the good housekeeper, die in a spotless home. It looks pretty clean to me, but then, I never did have high standards on that front.

I quickly return to the astral and move to the level her son is now residing on. It's an intermediate plane, for those still in transition, and not that far, actually, from where Reid is resting. But whereas Reid's rest home is very similar to the countryside bed and breakfasts he's used to on his bike travels, the boy is staying with some acquaintances of mine who often take in troubled teenagers, as their residence has the required patina of trendy urban decay that so charms the young habitués of chill-out rooms of the new-style dance palaces. On Earth he was just your average hormonally imbalanced bag of reckless energies, neither wicked nor wonderful, merely obsessed with his stage in life. Now he's remorseful and beginning to reach inside himself for reasons. I find him in the garden reading. Well, that's a step forward.

I quickly relate the drama at hand, sensing that the urgency of the situation could make good use of his remorse. And indeed it does. In fact he is thrilled to think that he can help. To think that he is being allowed to help. As a fairly new arrival, he cannot distinguish the tuggings of his mother's grief from his own overwhelming sense of futility and seems genuinely shocked by my news. In this, of course, he is quite typical of the self-obsession of the teenage years. Just shifting the burden of his confusions from the physical to the astral does little to lessen them.

He allows himself to sink into the safety of my expertise, and we shift levels and arrive in the kitchen. He is immediately affected and rushes to his mother's side, who is now engaged, rather innocuously, in washing up the breakfast dishes. If I were not so inured to such scenes I would find it heartbreaking to watch the boy's anguished attempts at consolation. He flutters around her, frantically trying to make contact. I can see the flurry of his emotions is just confusing the issue and pull him back to the other side of the room, where I attempt to calm him and get him to join me in projecting thoughts of love and serenity towards the mother, who is now directing her efforts at the floor.

Our combined efforts have anything but the effect intended: The mother stops her cleaning to weep again, recalling, as far as I can make out, some happy day from the boy's childhood. I lead him into the other room and try to explain the situation. At first he seems thrilled by the prospect of imminent reunion. I wisely refrain from saying anything about misery loving company and go on to explain that it may not be that simple, that gloom can cast a barrier thicker even than that between the physical and astral, but my efforts fall on rather deaf ears.

The house has a clammy, syrupy atmosphere that I'm beginning to find quite distasteful, but the boy still seems happy enough. God knows, it was easy enough for him to shuck his troubles and speed into what seems an easier existence. Why shouldn't his mom join him if she feels so shitty? Who the heck am I to tell him otherwise? Kids got no respect these days.

I change the subject and ask about grandparents. Yes, two of them are dead. Just what we need; I smile, hoping that they were not alcoholics like the last two I tried to use. Lord, I couldn't even get them to leave the divey bar they were hanging out in, waiting, with a mighty selection of so-called friends, for some drunken incarnate to slip out of his shell so that they can scrabble over who gets to go in and feel the intoxication. It's all so grimy and pathetic, but at the same time desperately funny if you can momentarily disconnect.

I leave the boy sitting on a couch, zip back to the astral and put out a call. Of course, there are precious few grannies that actually look like grannies here. A conventionally pretty woman of indeterminate age approached me. Telepathy as person-to-person telephone calls again. It seems magical at first, but when you've been here a while, you take it for granted, as you on Earth do the phone.

The woman tells me she has already spent a good deal of energy trying to cheer up her daughter but now feels it's hopeless. She wonders, somewhat accusingly, why I don't already know this, if I'm such a whiz kid. In fact I do but have tried to take a more positive approach. Her aura says sloth, selfishness, and toadying envy vying with anger: I should've known better.

She fades from view and I return to the house in time to see the bathwater running. I can't believe the son wants to watch this, but he does, and without much emotion. She does the usual razor on the wrist, and we all watch the water turn red. There's a ghoulishness to the son's interest that makes me wonder about the number of horror movies watched and the hypnotizing effect of lower astral vibrations.

Sure enough, as she's ebbing away, a motley crew of wanna-be demons shows up, looking for fresh meat. The atmosphere of gloom and depression draws them like flies. They saunter and creep like a group of ten-year-old boys trying to fondle lingerie on a washing line. Their clothes are tattered and their attitudes shabby; I scare them away with a couple of flashes of bright light. It's an easy trick once you've mastered it, and let me tell you, it works like a charm every time. It even stirs the son, who immediately wants to know how I did it.

His "How'd you do that, man?" seems somewhat incongruous in the context of his dying mother, but that's teenagers for you. Just changing planes doesn't do a thing for anyone's intelligence, we all know that, but the truism applies equally to taste and decorum. You don't always meet the best type of people in this line of work, that's for sure.

I tell him I'll explain later, and we watch the astral form of his mother appear above her wilting flesh. She is still encased in gloom but her son's excitement soon restores her to a level I can work with. I experience the strange reunion with mixed emotions.

It's very unprofessional for me to have emotions at all. My skills generally require the tact and demeanor of a highly polished maitre d' who can glide through the most awkward of situations with barely a ripple of discomfort. Amidst tears of joy and laughter, so bizarre above a still-warm corpse, I lead my charges on.

Using the tried and true hand-holding method, which minimizes the risk of any rubbernecking pit stops in the lower astral, we returned to the boy's temporary residence. It was probably as good a place as any for them right now. Bob and Carole met us in their rose garden, where, as they tended to their flower beds, three young men serenaded them with their acoustic guitars. Bob grinned in welcome and I could sense he was grateful that they hadn't yet asked about electricity in the afterlife. Plenty of time for that later, he seemed to be thinking.

Mother and son stood shyly back, engrossed in each other, as I made what they took to be arrangements. Bob and Carole's was for suicide or sudden-death teenagers, but they kept a couple of spare rooms for relatives, and sure enough both of them were currently empty. Carole sensed the situation and invited them in for a cup of tea. The newly dead mother didn't seem to think this sudden invitation at all incongruous, so simple was her transition.

Wonder no more why suicide was so frowned upon in earlier times. No one would have stayed physical if they'd realized how easy it was in Heaven. Yes, fear of damnation had a purpose once.

I chatted with Bob a while and listened politely to the jamming guitars. Like all young men everywhere, they sought approval. And I wouldn't mind betting that lack of approval from parents played a large part in their fall from grace.

Ah life! What a grand experiment in form and expression!

I made an informal departure, citing other pressing duties. The young men nodded sagely and Bob let go a twinkle. I think he guessed my plan.

A Little R and R

I transferred to my own locale and settled, without too much thought, by the stream that enlivened what you on Earth might consider my backyard. And really, to be fair, it's not that different from one of those suburban backyards that trail off into a few acres of unspoiled bush, ravines, and rivers that I've noticed on some of my trips back in the last few years.

That earlier penchant, so common during my last sojourn, for flattening all in the name of progress, democracy, and profit seems to have been superseded by a desire to blend with nature. Settling against a tree trunk, I bathed myself in the atmosphere of gurgling, whispering, and caressing.

Imagine your favorite park on a quiet Sunday summer morning, your daily worries suddenly without any weight, and your face warmed by a June sun. Now imagine, if you can, the tender pleasure of that magnified into quiet, sustaining ecstasy. Do not be ashamed to use post-orgasmic serenity if you wish, for it certainly conveys some, although not all, of the surpassing ease I wish to convey.

Surrounded by sentient forms that whisper and tinkle, I drift detached, my activities suspended. Needless to say it is pure delight. Those of you who've ingested the magic mushroom on Earth may smile when I use words like whisper and tinkle, as that is an aspect of the mushroom experience.

I had the opportunity to so ingest in my last year of "life," on a visit to California to taste what has become known to the nation as "Beat" culture. Veronica had once again run to Reid, bemoaning an excess of stability, and I had run west in a desperate effort to prove I wasn't so completely boring. In a club to hear some cool West Coast jazz, I met up with a man who, recognizing the incipient pilgrim under the mask of a mature accountant on a mad fling, took me under his wing. A week later, under the protection of the giant redwoods in the north of the state, I tasted the transcendence offered by the mushroom.

I later insisted the forest had "spoken to me," and we fell to discussing the Christian notion of "speaking in tongues." But it was only when I passed over, later that same year, and tasted the fruits of the astral that I began to see the connection. Certain psychoactive compounds raise the human consciousness from the physical to the boundaries of the astral, or perhaps they just dissolve the filters that keep the vibrant universe at bay, but don't go telling anyone I told you, or you'll be castigated for promoting drug use amongst the young and impressionable.

How Channeling Looks from This Side

Since I "died" in 1963 there's been an upsurge in all things spiritual, channeling amongst them. In the previous century it had become known as mediumship and spiritualism, and as such I had checked it out during a couple of summer vacations. Prone to all kinds of quackery, it had become somewhat disreputable by the postwar period, and I must admit I rather chuckled at it until my sister Ann disappeared from "life" in a series of quite unexpected heart attacks. She was only a few months old and I felt God must have had a reason to deprive my parents of a great joy. My poor mother was likely devastated, though I had to sneak behind her pride and dignity to even guess that. I thought it must've been like losing your best friend, as stupid as that may sound now. Years later, I would whisper her name under the covers, convinced we would've made a much happier couple than Veronica and I. But it wasn't until I hit the spirit world, with its much wider vistas, that I fully understood the depth of the enigma, not to mention my odd behavior. As Yankee families go, we were as repressed and eccentric as they come.

Now, of course, I know she just removed her coat and stepped on the elevator for the next floor in the great Bloomingdale's of life, but back then I thumbed my nose at all such easy answers. They were just too damned easy, and besides, they didn't help the pain I was feeling. She even appeared in dreams and told me as much. I'd wake up wondering why she looked so radiant and cheery, and wiser even than the wise child is supposed to be, and then I'd go through the rest of the day trying to forget.

She was so happy because she was here. And now that I've been here a while, I can't say I blame her. These Elysian Fields are hard to beat.

And where is she now, I hear some of you asking. Well, she's readying for rebirth if you must know. She left this plane, and the Phoebe personality, a while back, up through the spheres back to the godhead, the absolute, the undifferentiated void, whatever your tradition likes to call it.

She wants to be a baby again. God, I don't envy her task, but she was determined to be of service, and one can hardly fault that. I just thought it was too soon, that she needed more time to digest and reflect. More time, I recall her laughing. She was right, I was being absurd. Besides, her mission would be of short duration.

She is, in fact, a fetus now, floating in and out of the womb of her choice. An artificial insemination job, and not quite the genes she'd prefer. But you take what comes your way. The women she's being born to are old companions from way back. One of their guardians came with a proposal: that she might take a short incarnation to shake them out of their materialism. It wouldn't be much, went the argument, just a few short months of breast-feeding and burping and she'd be back here in a jiffy. I'd been dead too long to know what a separatist feminist was, but apparently they're a potent blend of dead suffragettes and World War II soldiers out to clear the planet of industrialists and powerful men generally.

Good luck to all of them, ablaze with their agendas! Sounds like a risky venture to me. But whatever happens, I'll be here when she gets back. That's love for you. And as for my first day dead, Ann tricked me by appearing as the beautiful Phoebe and making me just beg for a date before she let on. And yes, that's love for you, too.

I've wandered somewhat from my theme, how channeling looks from this side. Well, it looks like a wandering light, which, when you follow it to its source, turns out to be a deeply contemplative or meditating human being, filled with a desire for illumination.

One of best transcribers is Audrey, whose socioeconomic profile is as follows: a divorced mother of two, living precariously with her teenagers in small town in Oregon. Besides being an accomplished and caring massage therapist, she belongs to a coven of self-professed white witches, specializing in healing rituals of one kind or another.

She took up automatic writing pretty much on a whim, and her regular guardian presence, an old chum of mine who prefers the name Farley, not really being of a philosophical bent, referred the case to me. I, being an arrogant sort who figures he's got the universe all figured out, found it was an offer I couldn't refuse. Hey, I've spent ages hanging out on the mental plane with lots of heavy hitters, I've got plenty of that uplifting manna to move.

Here's an example of the sort of thing we started with. Audrey would, after ten minutes of meditation, sit in front of the TV with the sound turned off and pen and paper in hand. She would then pose a question, to which I, being right beside her, both in space and spirit, would instantly reply. I think her biggest surprise was how quickly I answered. It took her months to get over it.

How is consensus reality created?
Through tacit agreement among the participants.
On all levels this is true?
On all levels of form. In the formless worlds that lie beyond, it is impossible to tell the created from the creator, so although the same truth holds, it would seem impossible to verify.
On which level of consciousness exists this tacit agreement?
In the superconsciousness, that of the higher self.

Is there any particular reason for this level being used?

Yes. At that level all sentient beings can instantly communicate across any barriers of species or culture. Also at that level the agreement can be maintained without disturbing the free will and natural progress of body and soul.

So the higher self understands the usefulness of submitting to these collective illusions and permits the soul's submergence in them?

Yes, absolutely. It's much like throwing yourself in the deep end to see how well you adapt to floating.

As she gazed at the moving images between questions, this exchange took over an hour. An increasing lack of self doubt streamlined later efforts.

Farley usually keeps an eye on things while I set to work. You'd be amazed at the succession of bedraggled critters who come by and try to muscle in on the action. Despite an array of pleading, imploring looks, they have little or nothing of value to impart to a suffering humanity. Mostly because they are mired in suffering themselves. Make no mistake, they have a breast to beat and will do so at the slightest glimmer of attention. Pathetic astral shells they may be, but you still have to chase them off with a stick, if you know what I mean.

Anyway, that's Farley's job. I stick to the broadcasting. Come to think of it, they are not unlike the drifters and beggars I see in the warm underground tunnels of your big cities, in that they can barely maintain the veneer of civility for more than a few seconds. When their pleading is not met with indulgence they can quickly turn ugly.

On one recent visit, while Farley kept the crowds at bay, I communicated the following:

Between Lives in the Formless Worlds

Dwelling in the light of the higher self, that undifferentiated ocean of tenderness that is, in itself, just a bubble in a larger ocean, is a bliss beyond recognition. We bathe in its ecstatic vibrations for eternity, knowing that being is all.

And yet we tire of the inactivity, of being a universe in potential, endlessly preparing for new aspects of perfection. We crave fresh knowledge of ourselves. And so, like bored sunbathers on a perfect summer afternoon, we kick ourselves out of this Heaven and heave towards yet another incarnation, where, once again, form will find us plenty of excuses for activity, and ego will assure us of significance and meaning.

It appeared on her writing pad just as I purveyed it, which is something of an accomplishment, as in our early days of communication, she would sometimes get things quite muddled and I would blame myself.

Anyway, it appeared sometime later in her monthly newsletter under the pen name "Solana."

I was pleased with the success of these short transmissions and set about a more complicated task, the telling of a murder story from this side of things. For this one I put my best literary foot forward.

Don't ask her how she knows. She doesn't even know herself. All she knows is that she knows.

There is no doubt, of that she is certain. She awaits her fate with a patience she has never known before. She used to be just a little girl, growing in the usual way. Getting an inkling for rebellion, trying out her mother's cosmetics in the bathroom.

I was with her many times during the last few weeks. Watching and waiting, humming a little tune. It was one of the few cases I've covered where the soul's knowing has penetrated the ego's activity. Most people are so caught up in the excitement of their various adventures, when that seeming hand of fate executes its instructions, the ego resists and rebels.

She is, of course, a bit of the wise old soul in the twelve-year-old body, and that's a good part of the reason. She entered that life with certain karmic agreements, as we all do. One of those agreements was willing sacrifice. Another was an attempt to lift someone's darkness with her light. A third was to spark some growth in the souls of her parents, both of whom wanted to escape the rut of convention they'd carved in too many lives.

I was among those who counseled her before birth. I was quite new to the role at the time and really only sat in to listen and learn. But around her tenth year Earth time, I was nominated by Elise, the spirit in charge, to take over. She said I was ready.

I approached the girl in the dream world. She saw me as a glowing guardian angel, and I saw it as wise not to disabuse her of the notion. Whatever those incarnate are comfortable with, that's the watchword. The parents, who, of course, also needed counseling, saw me as a bespectacled and bemused financial adviser, not unlike the temperate accountant I once was.

I basically reminded them all of the transience of the upcoming tragedy and their earlier commitment to it. Usually, in these cases, as I was to discover with experience, the incarnates cannot remember your discussions with them from night to night. Some of them can be appallingly vague and distracted. The girl, though, showed great promise. Through earlier efforts in other incarnations, the link between soul and ego had been strengthened, and some information would stick.

I tuned into her thoughts in the daytime and could see she was mulling over her mortality, albeit in a conventionally religious way. A very joyful, loving soul, the plan was to bring her together with a sadist of long standing, to see if her light might raise his vibration.

A, shall we say, repeat offender, with a grim family and karmic background, he moved to her neighborhood after a custody battle, which uncovered scars on psyche as well as body. A centuries-old desire for vengeance settled on him once more. It came to him as surely as grace to a devout religionist. Flies on jam, etc., etc.

The girl and he had been, apparently, enemies and rivals a couple of times in the past. I say apparently, as I hadn't checked out the details myself but had been given the understanding by Elise when she handed me the file, as it were.

Rick, as we shall call him here, pursued the bar-after-work lifestyle and the hapless, lonely women he met there. A charming veneer allowed him a certain sway with their sexual favors, but his innate aggressiveness and will to dominate soon scared them away. His binge drinking quickly attracted the usual host of desperate discarnates, eager to displace him in the drunken body when he slipped out unconscious.

Watching them, as I did from time to time, was not unlike coming across a group of seagulls in a parking lot, squawking and diving at some precious french fries. I briefly merged with one of them, and while fighting off my revulsion at his spiritual stinkiness, I did feel his deep pleasure at the sudden immersion in the sea of alcoholic vibes. The best comparison I can make is that of a dirty hobo long denied a hot, fragrant bath.

The most persistent of the discarnates was also a belligerent career psychopath, who easily latched onto his vengeful tendencies, lapping up all the subsequent arguments and fights with glee.

On one particularly long binge this grim excuse for a gentleman made himself most comfortable in his host and would not budge at the end of the "blackout." His host, of course, had no idea of his new guest, as their tastes in life were more or less the same.

Such a coexistence on the Earth plane is not uncommon. Some of them, in fact, are almost benign. They do, of course, retard the evolution of the souls involved but do not, in the larger measure of things, cause any great harm. This coupling, however, was to prove as explosive and, ultimately, creative as any I've been involved with.

Here is where the first part of the channeling ended. It was published as is. Unfortunately, another young girl was similarly dispatched the next week not fifty miles away, and the editors felt it prudent to drop the next installment in case some crime and punishment fundamentalists got a hold of it. An unsolved but much-rumored bombing of an abortion clinic had cast a shadow over all new-age idealism.

Here is the planned second installment.

I write with the "murdered" girl at my side. She smiles her greetings to all her Earth-bound mourners and asks you all to restrain your grieving as it blocks the path of her progress as clouds do the sun, although she understands and forgives you if you can't bring yourself to do it.

I met her at the moment of her departure from the physical. Her tormentor lay in a heap below us, his rage spent and his remorse raging. I held a sobbing child in my arms and looked at the illusion of devastation. I've been doing this type of transition long enough to know that the fear and violence of the Earth should no longer affect me, but sometimes I am swayed. I of all people should know that all tragedy leads to eternal life, but I felt myself slipping into the trance, so as much for myself as my charge I whisked us away to a reception area which my companion will describe:

"It was the most beautiful place I have ever seen, better even than the Bahamas, which I used to think was the best. Everything glowed like it had little lights in it, even the people looked like they were lit up inside. A lovely lady took me to my room and talked to me about life at the hotel. It was a special children's hotel where you got up anytime you wanted and ate anything you liked, even if it was just bubble gum. We looked out the window and I could see all these children from all over the world playing in the pool and the garden next to it.

"And then she showed me my closet, which had all these lovely party dresses and shoes and really cool T-shirts and halter tops. She said there was gonna be a party tomorrow night for somebody's birthday and I said was I invited and she said she'd make sure I was.

"She asked me if I wanted to try out the bed, and I thought well, why not. And it was like the softest thing ever. As soon as I lay on it I felt sleepy. Usually I can sit up all night watching TV, but there it was all different. The lady lay down beside me and we talked about this and that. I asked about my mum and dad. She said we could go visit them later. I told the lady that I always had a drink before I went to bed, and she asked me if chocolate milk would be okay. I said sure, and she went away to get it. I was asleep before she got back. That bed was just magic. I know because the glass of chocolate milk was still there when I woke up.

"The next day was just a blast. I don't know when I've ever had more fun. I made a lot of new friends in no time, and two different boys asked me to go to the party with them. Peter I met in the swimming pool. He lived in Boston before he got this tumor beside his brain that he said was as big as an apple. I believe him; a kid in my school was just the same, and he died, too. Andy was passing out the juice and pop at lunch and asked me where I was from. He'd been in a car accident with his grand-father somewhere in Connecticut. Anyway, we all went to the party together and danced and danced and danced. You just never get tired here.

"After things got cleared away and I went back to my room to get changed and maybe watch a video (there was a whole shelf to chose from), Henry, who is still next to me now, came by and said if I felt like it, now was a good time to visit with my folks.

"We had a little talk before we got there. He told me how excited they'd be to see me again, and that they might get so excited they'd disappear and go right back to their bodies, and if they did I was not to be too upset, as we could visit the next time they were asleep.

"We floated around my old neighborhood, just to get the hang of it, and then Henry went ahead, to give them a little warning. I waited in the back garden, by the swing set that daddy built for me when I was little and that my little brother now used. Funny, with all the excitement I'd forgotten about him. Then I felt kinda bad, but what use does an eleven-year-old girl have for a three-year-old boy? I know that sounds terrible, but we just lived different lives, that's all.

"Mum and Dad looked pretty much like they usually do. And boy, were they happy to see me! I've never had so many hugs! Mum shouted something like 'I knew it! I knew it! See I told you, Dan!' Dad looked a bit ashamed but still really happy. Mum just hugged me and cried and laughed. Henry stood next to Dad and kinda threw a glow around him. I don't know how he did it, but I could see it over Mum's shoulder. Henry told me later he was trying to dissipate the cloud of rage Dad felt for the man who attacked me with feelings of forgiveness.

"Henry said that they would have trouble understanding that I was dead when they saw me like that, and I could really understand what he meant because I had a lot of trouble understanding that myself. I felt more alive than ever, just so bubbly and, I dunno, full. Nothing like what you imagine dead to be. Mum and Dad were more like the kids that had to be calmed down.

"Anyway we talked for what seemed like ages. I told them all about the hotel and the kids there and how much fun I was having. When it was time to go I thought Mum would never let go of me. Dad had to sort of tug at her. Henry said we'd be able to meet again very soon and insisted we say 'au revoir' instead of 'goodbye.'"

This last portion of the ongoing transmission was shared only with Audrey's coven of white witches. The plan was to publish it later at some more inconspicuous date. None of her colleagues seemed very surprised at the revelations. It was rather like preaching to the converted. Of course, there are small groups of souls all over the planet who understand the karmic causes of tragedies and the large discrepancy between a soul's agenda and the ego's reaction to it. We, on this side, only wish those groups were larger and more influential.

I returned with my charge to the children's hotel, where, despite all manner of alluring activities, she announced she was ready for bed. I saw no reason to dissuade her, and wishing her a well-deserved rest, which on those very special beds I knew she would undoubtedly get, I pantomimed a very dignified departure which coaxed the giggle I'd guessed was ready.

Its success rather spurred me on: After reporting her rest period to Meryl, who'd shown her around earlier, and would now, as you say on Earth, keep an eye on her, I decided to go for one of my little nocturnal adventures.

Dead Drunks

It would still be the middle of the night on the West Coast, so there I headed, making a pit stop in the Rockies to enjoy the various views, not to mention the company of the great devas who brood like mother hens on that noble range.

Interesting characters, devas: You don't so much communicate with them as bathe in them. Which, in a way, is not unlike a city, that most human of habitations.

I swooped down into Seattle, whizzing up and down side streets just for fun. The seedier neighborhoods are the best bet for the type of soul rescue I had in mind. The strays one finds are usually so befuddled with booze and dope and befogged with fear and ignorance that there's little, if anything, you can do to ease their passage. Lifetimes of self-pitying obsessiveness usually render them impermeable to all but the lowest vibrations. But, once in a while, a young soul just skirting the shores of self-abasement can be nudged in a new direction.

I spied a young drunk stumbling out of a bar and into a dark side street, where he was almost immediately set upon by two slightly less inebriated men for the remains of his paycheck. The blow to his skull was brutally and instantaneously successful, so while his physical self lay prone on the sidewalk, the astral continued its stumbling in a perfect imitation of its fleshy counterpart.

I tried the "Hey buddy, you're dead!" routine from a couple of angles, unfortunately to little effect. It rarely works, but it doesn't take a moment to give it a try. And like you say on Earth, where there's life there's hope. He heard someone shouting, but it sounded like a series of barks, and the actual words failed to penetrate his consciousness.

My next effort was to impersonate a kindly hooker. I've been a courtesan in a couple of lives (Imperial Rome and Renaissance Venice) and the sexual mothering of men comes quite easily to me. Let's face it, it's an act, just like any other.

I manifested the form of an alluring slattern, somewhat more glamorous, admittedly, than the average for the area, which was your basic bedraggled crack fiend fishing for another hit.

This time I let him see rather than hear me. Still assuming he was alive and drunk, he blundered over, making what he thought was sense. I smiled and asked if he needed a place to rest his head for the night. Money was not mentioned; he could not believe his luck.

In a vacant lot I made a thought form of a decrepit house, complete with a half rotted porch and shabby blinds. Can you see the dog-pawed door with its loose pane of pebbled glass? I let him slump on the tatty couch and poured us some drinks. In such situations I have discovered that any amber colored liquid will do. While I suspect he was more of a bourbon man, mine tasted more or less like tequila.

We toasted each other's health, and giving him plenty of opportunity to be hypnotized by my lovely legs, I sat on his lap and draped myself around him. Again the impression was "Can't believe my luck."

I could feel he was a young, naive, and trusting soul who'd often been deceived by conniving buddies. I was about to turn something of the same trick upon him, only I had his best interests at heart. I was conducting a divine deception.

Caressing his neck with little kisses, I played my tongue around his ear. Feeling a catlike purr of contentment, I whispered, "Listen honey, don't you know you're dead?"

"Dead drunk, more like."

"No sweetie. I mean it, you're a goner."

"Where am I then?"

"You're in the afterlife, that's where."

"And the afterlife is filled with total babes like you, right? Gees, if only I'd known."

A small but insistent ripple of sexual inadequacy surfaced in his dulled consciousness. I told him I was a bit more like Florence Nightingale than a total babe. He said I could've easily fooled him. Little did he know.

He'd once seen a stripper do that as her act. I told him I didn't strip. He said that was okay, a bird in the hand was worth two in the bush.

I rewarded him with a giggle; he seemed pleased and asked for another drink. I uncoiled myself with the charming compliance he craved. His level of gratification was something to behold. I held out his drink, but just out of reach. He gazed at me, contented as a baby just burped.

"Come," I wiggled my fingers, "I've got something to show you."

He seemed reluctant to move from his perch, but I moved to the rattletrap door with enough swish from the hip to bait him. I made sure he saw me float down the three steps to the sidewalk.

"Now see if you can do that!"

"No bloody way, I'll kill myself!"

"Can't be done dude, you're already dead."

"So you say. Man, am I confused." He sat down on the top step, his head in his hands.

"Come here, I've got something to show you. Come on, you don't have to float."

He grunted his dissatisfaction and, in standing up, fell forward into my arms. I steadied him easily and turned him around to face the house. "Now watch this," I ordered, dispersing the thought form as quickly as I'd created it. We stared at the vision of a weedy vacant lot.

"How the hell . . ."

"Did I do that? I'm a magician. Now watch this." Sensing his dream car, I created a thought form of a Corvette Stingray. A red one at that. And quick as a bunny hopped in. "Come on, I'll take you for a ride."

He kind of fell, face first, into the passenger seat, where I rearranged him with a couple of quick tugs. Still not knowing he was dead and therefore light as a feather, he looked at me in complete disbelief. I laughed and we motored away.

When we lifted off into the air he seemed no more surprised than before, which was good. I've had people try to bail out when I've pulled this stunt before, and the balletic maneuvers necessary to repossess them flipped them out more than ever.

We drove through a night sky and into a gradual dawn on one of the reception planes, and then right into the driveway of a rest home for dead drunks, ones that are considered salvageable.

Unbelievably, even for me who is used to these things, we were met by his sister, also a dead drunk, but one well on the way to recovery.

"Billy, Billy, oh God, it's so great to see you!"

"Vera, what are you doing here?"

"Waiting for you, you useless slimeball!"

Apparently, Billy had neglected to show up at his sister's wedding some years back. He claimed to have fallen in love on the way with a woman he met on the train, who convinced him to stop off in Vegas for the night, where they lost their collective shirts, such as they were. This I gleaned from their shoulder-shoving joust and argy-bargy.

While they were at it, I dematerialized the car, so when Billy tried to point out the awesome vehicle he'd arrived in, Vera was quick to point out its absence. Seeing one of the assistants waving from the doorway, a former dope mule on the Beirut to Marseilles run, now content to be a more active cog in our conveyor belt of consciousness, I knew they'd be in good hands so I took my leave and headed back to that lovely cottage in the sky that I dreamt of so often when last in the flesh. It may not always be my home as I pass in and out of the physical perfecting my follies, but it's rapidly becoming my home away from home.

Belief Systems: 1

Having given examples of some of the more, shall we say, eccentric of my activities, perhaps now is a good time to pass on the type of experience the vast majority of humans have on passing through the planes.

Basically they die and continue on in a community of like-minded spirits much like the one they left behind on Earth. And though religious dogmas assert otherwise, on the astral plane there is an environment to suit every belief system. Every culture and subculture can discover its parameters, paradoxically laid bare and polished up to a shine. No one lacks an appropriate landscape in which to perpetuate their human performance. Which, when you think of it, is just like on Earth.

In terms of pure metaphysics, there is only energy at varying rates of vibration, which in turn result in varying levels of density.

In the end it all boils down to belief systems. Whether you realize it or not, you subscribe to a belief system. Whether it is one of the sects of the major religions or the skeptical materialism of the modern techno-logical man or some vibrant remnant of animistic tribalism in the third world, every individual arrives on the astral with a firmly entrenched belief system. Even a soul cocooned in the black egg of ignorance that dictates a comalike sleep, from which he may not awaken for decades, or perhaps centuries, is the pawn of a belief system.

Much of the recent NDE literature has emphasized the familial nature of the experience, and for many this is undoubtedly true. And let me tell you, on some levels the eager anticipation of the arrivals of Uncle Ted and Aunty Mary can be just as wearisome to long-time resi-dents as the excited chatter of young parents to those who have long passed that stage in the physical life cycle.

On other levels—generally the ones that people "sink to"—souls pursue obsessive behavior patterns, and their former loved ones find the patterns either tedious, embarrassing, or repulsive and elect not to follow them into that particular abyss. Imagine, if you will, a brother who progressed through small-time drug dealing into major heroin importation and addiction. If he moved to Paris and fell into the com-pany of thieving junkies and whores, he would not be any more distant from his respectable family than if he, as many do, took up residence in some lower astral slum with his like-minded compatriots, never for a moment seeing that the fate that has befallen them is one they have chosen.

These are but two examples of the endless variety of what I would call "communities of shared interests" on the astral. There are, in fact, as many as you can imagine, given the variety of activities on Earth, and it would take another book to document them all. And there are, in fact, large sociological documents in our libraries doing just that, but they are as massive as you might imagine, so I shall content myself with a representative sample.

To visit these communities without participating in their ongoing life can be compared to attending a large sporting event in which one has no intrinsic interest. While the players and audience are communing, enacting rituals that sustain their relationship, you watch bemused, wondering when the scales will fall from the eyes and the emperor will be seen as naked.

Let's start with the ones who refuse to recognize death. Of these there are two kinds: those who still wander the Earth plane, wondering why no one will talk to them, and others who mischievously/maliciously interfere with those who are, for them, quite deliciously unsuspecting.

On a quick reconnoiter through Anytown, U.S.A., we would find the following: dead alcoholics hanging around bars, waiting for heavy drinkers to pass out so they can fight over who gets into the vacated body; dead junkies hanging around crack houses and their high class counterparts, hoping for the same; dead johns hanging around brothels and escort agencies, looking to embrace the vibrations of lust; dead businessmen hanging about their old place of business, trying to influence the decision-making of their former colleagues; the odd dead pedophile hanging around a schoolyard, gloating but getting nowhere; dead sports fans hanging around stadiums and arenas, waiting for games; dead busybodies hanging around hospitals, amusing themselves with the endless ghoulish soap operas unfolding on every floor.

Now all these types have their guardian spirits ready to guide them onward to the "real" afterlife, but having developed either some hidebound materialist stance or some obsessive behavior pattern effectively gluing them to self-gratification, they are unable to see or hear the lighted beings beckoning them, and they continue on their rounds shrouded in the gloomy gray fog that is the emanation of their ignorance.

Such souls, being so self-obsessed, rarely form what we would call a community, but they do form a kind of psychic bridge to that first level of astral communities which are generally formed by atheists and materialists, who, while denying all evidence of an afterlife, find themselves in some kind of endless dream in landscapes as bleak as their imaginings. Though often quite prideful and self-centered, some of these folk, while developing their intellects on Earth, absorbed varying degrees of what has come to be known as secular humanism, and as this has bred in them the value of helping others, they tend to band together and "make the best of it."

Although I am reclining comfortably in the cottage as I dictate this to Gordon, my protégé and "author" of this work, let me now take you over to one of these communities. First of all, I step down my energy level (i.e., vibration) to something more suitable for the lower astral, else I'll scare them off by looking like a large floodlight. Explaining how I accomplish this is no easy task, but the phrase "attitude adjustment" seems useful. And yes, it is quite like the sprucing up of one's clothes and emotions that is undergone when coming home from work, feeling tired and grouchy, when one is reminded of a dinner party one cannot escape.

Here we go: The terrain is bleak, rugged, and windswept. And that would be a generous description. A slate gray sky of formless clouds that suggests the word November; some ancient stone hovels, crumbling and damp, are surrounded by wooden shacks of a more recent vintage; tufts of tenacious grass sprout from hard-packed soil; a scattering of large, menacing boulders suggests some prehistoric upheaval.

I stroll the lane that threads through the huts. The cold of a winter twilight seems to have shut in any inhabitants. I knock on a door. A ragged old man peers at me suspiciously.

"I suppose you'll be wanting to come in. Well, come in quick before I freeze."

I slip in and sit, as shown, by the fire. The stool I'm sitting on looks like it was carved sometime before the Renaissance. The old fellow settles on a rickety old rocking chair. I ask him how he's doing.

"As well as can be expected in this Hellhole. I expect you're as full of nonsense as usual."

He looked as though he wished he had the nerve to spit derisively into the fire. But no, that was not him, that was the type he used to employ. Bastards. How he used to long to be free of their incessant demands.

I assure him of his thought: "Yes, I've come to bore you with my brain-dead drivel, as you once so felicitously put it."

He indulged me with the bleakest and briefest of grins. I'd noticed a penchant for self-deprecating humor on my last visit. He looked for all the world like some down-and-out character from Dickens. The world had disgusted him and now he was stuck in some kind of repulsive dream that refused to go away.

"You say this is all a dream and I'm just some figment of a demon here to annoy you. What if I were to show you a better dream, one where fair damsels danced and sang in flower gardens, and delight is as eternal as despair is here?"

He hurrumphed a sneering snort that great actors would've admired. Underneath my serious demeanor I was mightily entertained. I had hoped that the image suggested, of fair damsels doing their bit in diaphanous gowns, would undermine his crustiness, but it was not to be, at least not this time.

I was accused of deceit. I was accused of wasting his time. I was denounced as dead. Demurring, I was challenged to prove my existence. I stepped up and pinched him firmly in the forearm. He yelped and cursed.

"Why you insolent whelp, how dare you!"

"Oh, how I've longed to be called an insolent whelp!"

"And now you mock me!" His face, not to mention his aura, reddened. He moved to strike me with his cane. I dodged the blow, laughing. He growled and returned to his seat, like the arthritic old man he thought he was.

"See you later, old fellow!" My cheek enraged him, as I knew it would, but it would help to chip away at his hardened shell of denial in a way that politeness wouldn't.

I crossed the lane to another ancient stone hut, where I knew a young man would be huddled under a blanket, scribbling away at his calculations. There was no point knocking, he would never respond. Something of a brilliant mathematician, he'd suffered a stroke while studying and barely noticed his passing. Concerned only for his work and the glory it might bring him, selfish ambition had combined with the atheism of his upbringing to plop him down here, where the desolation of the heart is mirrored in the landscape.

I sat down at the table across from him and gave out a warm hello; he glanced up briefly. Many pages covered in calculations littered the table. I sensed that he believed he was on the verge of some great breakthrough and that to break off from his line of thought would be catastrophic. Of course the complexity of this work would only be appreciated by other mathematicians, and as that would involve the sort of transformative journey only I, or someone like me, could instruct him in, his upcoming quandary seemed all too palpable. I waited, wondering how many visits would be necessary before the cockles of his heart began to warm.

Just then two familiar faces leered in at the door. A couple of teenage hoodlums racing away from their last robbery, now reduced to harassing other poor souls deep in denial. I manifested a very real-looking pistol and waved it in their faces. They turned and ran, still complete neophytes to the postmortem technologies of mind, doubtless to pursue further torments.

Our mathematician had not noticed.

"Ah, don't you worry about them, Hartz, they won't be back anytime too soon." That got him: He looked up puzzled. How did I know his name? The same way I knew everything else about him—his unaffectionate Marxist parents; his pretty but ditsy wife; his sad, ignored children; his fierce obsession with math—by merging my mind with his. A mental extension of empathy, it's easy once you know how.

I could see him wavering. How did I know his name? Was I worth the interruption? Was I merely a figment of this dream life, his rationalization of postmortem consciousness?

"You've been here before, haven't you?"

"Yes I have, Hartz."

"How do you know my name? No one here knows that, not the fellow who brings the firewood or the old lady who fetches tea and bread."

"That's because they're too polite to ask."

"It's appropriate for servants, I believe."

"The key word there is believe. They are who you believe they are."

"On the contrary, belief does not enter into it. Beliefs are for peasants who like to think superstitions are a thing of the past."

"They are not for someone like you who spends all his time working in an abstract symbolic language that can only be understood by other members of your tiny tribe, none of whom you can currently find."

"Of none of whom I am currently in need."

"And when you are, where will they be?"

"In my mind, where they always are."

"Ah, so you believe you have a mind?"

"I know so."

"And I suppose you have some elaborate proof of that theorem?"

"No more than you have an elaborate proof for yours. It's not something I have to prove. It's something I know."

"Just as I know you're dead?"

"Enough of your chatterings! I have work to do."

And with that his head was bowed and his blanket pulled tighter about his shoulders. I promised to return but he ignored me. He might be here for years, Earth time, before I could get through to him. The abstract beauty of pure mathematics had him in its grip, but like any intellectual studies when pursued for the gratification of the ego, it was as addictive as heroin and had many of the same results.

Come with me now to the scrabby forest not far from this Stone Age settlement (yes, it is that old). A wintry bleakness bares the trees. No one expects the leaves of spring here, and thus they never get them. Cold winds and dark mists alternate for atmosphere.

Dead hermits often repair here, carrying on their hiding and scavenging, as if just awakened from a long and dark sleep. They make new shelters with branches, twigs, and rags. And sit in them, brooding.

Wildlife such as squirrels, chipmunks, crows, and ravens have consented to come down from the beautiful forests of the summerland to cheer up these poor waifs. A couple of the little rascals dart about me now, much to my delight. They know why I'm here and they wish me well.

There's a crusty old fellow I want you to meet. A hater of humanity, he hides in these winter woods, living only for the squirrels who scatter his contempt with their carefree games. Although I am one of very few human visitors, he has yet to give me the time of day.

I squat outside his shack and wait. The squirrels appear and begin to dance about me. Hearing their activity, he peers out. I smile; he scowls. The squirrels dart in after him and I hear what can only be described as grunted chuckles.

Some squirrels reappear, jumping on my lap and shoulders. I act out my delight noisily. I see another disapproving scowl. This performance repeats itself until eye contact is established: merely a look that accompanies another scowl.

But my initial enthusiasm for a breakthrough in our stalemate turns out to be overly optimistic. It is obvious he is still not ready to be coaxed out of his dream. Perhaps next time.

I should probably be taking you to the rocky gorge on the far side of the forest, where you can see the results of skeptical materialism firsthand. But I am hearing a call from Reid, so let us return there momentarily and perhaps deal with his need.

Reid and Fiona

I find Reid splayed on the lawn, chatting with Fiona, one of the resident helpers. He thanks me for not being there when he first awakened, as I had threatened. I give him a quick hug and promise it'll never happen again. Fiona teases him mercilessly, reminding him he'd only been awake for a little over an hour before deciding he needed another nap.

Reid accuses her of exaggerating and we all laugh. When Fiona, at her own insistence, disappears to make some tea, I settle down beside him and ask how he is doing. "Not too shabby" is his reply. I ask him if he really feels dead yet.

Well, he thinks so. It had all come to a head less than an hour ago when he met one of his poker-playing buddies in the pool room of the guest house. Fiona had been showing him around when Fred appeared, cue in hand, ready to resume a game interrupted at least five years previously by a fire in a Denver apartment building.

Fred had just died of a heart attack right in the middle of an all-nighter in Don's basement rec room, but not before he'd heard of Reid's bike crash. Apparently Rick had been visiting his ex in Missouri, not ten minutes from where Reid took his fall. And wouldn't you know it, their eldest was first cop on the scene. Of course, everyone knew he'd been going cross country and had wondered whether he were still up to it, and of course, there'd been a couple of know-it-all-alongers nodding their heads.

Fred had been just about ready to throw in his two cents when he'd keeled over, right there in his seat. Jesus, you should have seen the commotion, just as he did while floating below the ceiling. He never knew dying could be so damn funny.

Fiona brought some tea on a tray and set it down beside them. Reid, true to form, did not move a muscle to help her. He had always managed to make his disdain for women work for him. I'd always suspected that was a big part of Veronica's attraction to him, being ignored, but now was not the time to bring that up.

But apparently it was: According to Fred, Veronica was organizing the funeral. And having long since left Reid's adventures for the safer ground of Gerald, the perennially successful stockbroker, now senile, she could easily afford the kind of lavish outlay he knew she would want. Not that he gave a shit, mind you, he'd be just as happy to continue traveling across the country, and as Fiona had told him there was no reason he shouldn't, he was now considering a trip round the globe.

He asked what I'd been up to. Since I died, or just recently? Whatever.

I described the scope of this narrative and the brief tour of the lower astral I'd just suspended for his benefit. Perhaps he'd care to come along?

The lower astral. Fiona'd just been talking about it. That was where all the fucked-up people were, right? Nah, he'd pass for now thanks, sounded too much like Detroit. Another time maybe. Hell, he was having too much fun here. At this he glanced significantly at Fiona, who reciprocated with an indulgent smile.

Fiona was not exactly a friend, but I knew her well enough; she would not be the pushover Reid expected. The women who worked in these guest homes were something like nurses, quite accustomed to their transient guests taking a shine. I finished my tea and, wishing them a good day, took my leave, pausing only to wave from the garden's edge and dramatically disappear once I'd gotten Reid's attention. That ought to keep him going for a while.

Belief Systems: 2

Okay, here we are, back at the edge of this primeval forest; the land turns scrubby and rocky, bleak and bare. A dark sky broods over this pathetic excuse for a landscape, as it has for who knows how long and as it will as long as the desiccated and hopeless souls who unknowingly sustain its creation need its backdrop for their dejection.

The longer we walk the more chilly and windswept it feels. A deep gorge opens up ahead. We peer into a gloomy canyon. I can tell you're not so keen to go down, but down we go, along a bumpy rocky path that seems cut from a wall of stone.

A sharp wind seems to cut and jab. Inhospitable is the mood of the moment. Finally, on the canyon floor, faced with giant boulders that loom up out of nowhere, and skipping over scuzzy little creeks you'd really rather not step in, we come across hunched and squatting figures, either looking dolefully into the middle distance or staring disconsolately at their feet. Notice how completely self-absorbed they are. Now look at the ones prostrate, or curling up against boulders. Truly, they are sleeping the sleep of the dead.

There are, as far as I have been able to discern, two kinds. Complete materialists whose brains would never admit the possibility of eternity, and that type of Christian who resolutely believes he will be awakened on Judgment Day. Of the Christians, only the most hard-hearted are here; those less willing to condemn are sleeping in hospital wards dotted throughout the astral, where a succession of helpers keep an eye on their slumbers.

Now we're coming up to the moaners. Hear that low wailing, more fit for the aftermath of disaster? It's a chorus of self-pity from those who would never believe in an afterlife but find themselves here full of regrets and complaints. Classic whiners, one and all. If you can get any of them to pay attention, which mostly you can't since they've convinced themselves you're but a demonic figment of something or other, all you'll get is a litany of woe, repeated ad infinitum if you're daft enough to stand there, as I was many Earth-years ago, full of naive missionary zeal.

Retrievals can be accomplished from such dire straits, but it usually takes tag teams of helpers stretched throughout the decades to deliver just one or two upwards and onwards. Let's keep moving.

Well, well, what have we here. It's a crushed car, driven over the cliff edge by those two hoodlums I scared off with the pistol earlier. My guess was they'd just committed a robbery in a stolen car, and crashing at high speed made such a swift transition they did not know they were dead. Probably after my rebuff they made a thought form of a getaway car, rode off in it to the cliff edge, and thinking they were still physical, created the thought form of the wreckage and their crushed bloody frames.

Notice the thought form of the car slowly disintegrating. See how the sad sight is slowly revealed: two battered bodies that were once boys now believing they have killed themselves. Let us leave them for now and go visit the cave dwellers. The rock face up ahead is as ancient as any in New Mexico or Arizona, and many of the dead have taken their turns dwelling there.

Right now there are quite a number of strict materialists who are willing, at least, to admit each other into their "dream." After all, they're dead, so what other option is there? For some there's a grim gallows humor in it all: Life had been a pain, and it didn't even have the decency to call it quits, it tortured you with all the random thrashing of brain activity. There are several here who will be glad to debate with you over the complete lack of independent verification for your "afterlife" theory. Prove to me it's not all a dream, they will say smugly.

But wait, what's that? It's one of my suicides calling. Let's move on up and see what the problem is.

Back at Bob and Carole's

As I approach I see Carole at her favorite pastime: rearranging the roses. She laughs when I tease her and says its easier than rearranging the furniture. She nods inside, indicating that my mother-and-son duo is eager to talk.

I meet them in the lounge area and immediately they are on me about past lives. Yes, I tell them, their suspicions are probably correct. They have spent many lives together, and yes, that is probably why she felt such an overwhelming urge to be with him this time.

Were they married before? Is it possible? Is it like incest? Will there be trouble? They gush with questions. Carole could've answered them, but she said they needed a man's authority, and she's probably right— she usually is. People arrive here with all, or at least most, of their prejudices intact, and we helpers, if we are indeed to help, must adjust to their peculiar needs.

If, for example, there'd been a dire need for a priest, or say a kindly social worker, then Carole would've summoned that character rather than me, but the boy had been wildly impressed with my abilities and doubtless felt I was a font of wisdom. Which, by his standards, is more or less true. But there are plenty like me around here.

And so as I reassured them of the wholesome nature of their binding love, I suggested that they relax, enjoy the atmosphere of the guest house, join in the recreations, and generally soak up the good vibes of their new neighborhood, and in a few days I would escort them to one of the karmic study centers in the city, where they could view at their leisure the variety of their past-life connections.

This seemed to satisfy them. Before taking my leave I asked the mother if she'd been drawn to her funeral yet. No, she blurted, she did not want to go, her son's was torture enough.

I told her that I sympathized with her desire to run from misery, but I warned her that resisting the pull of the longing and anxiety expressed by those she left behind might cause her more grief than submitting to it, and also she might do them all a favor by taking some of the love she felt on reuniting with her son and spreading it around to lessen the load.

I left them smiling, which is as much as you can ask for, isn't it? Then I got a call: time for a music lesson. I replied, yes, why not, it's probably just what I need.

A Music Lesson

My instructor, the ever-genial Gerard, was last seen on Earth in France at the turn of the century, in the guise of a postman in Avignon, a rather ordinary family man but for his weekend devotion to the works of Debussy.

The highlight of his short life, or so I've been told, was two weeks in Paris, going to concerts and galleries and listening to Eric Satie play in a sidewalk cafe.

He's likely just finished with some chamber music recital and wants to kick back and relax, and what better way to relax than watch me flounder over the rhythmic subtleties of Satie's *Gnossiennes* and *Gymnopedies*.

Which, without fail, I do. I'm not the most musical of souls but I'm trying. On the harpsichord too, which, for Satie, is something of an innovation.

Gerard says I'm getting better. I laugh and say I notice he doesn't cringe quite so much as he used to. He wants me to move on to some of the simplest preludes of Debussy. When I reply, "All in good time sir, all in good time," he chuckles, knowing I'm apprehensive.

Gerard assures me that one day I shall be as fluent as he in the musical idiom of his beloved France. Delicacy can be deciphered, he reminds me with a wink, before embracing in the traditional Gallic manner and excusing himself. He must go, he says, to visit his children, both recently dead and still adjusting—his daughter to being young and beautiful and minus the misogynist husband, and the son to the vacation-like idleness. And, he remembers at the door, would I like to hear new works by Ravel and Poulenc?

Well, there's no refusing an offer like that, even here, where any concert's but a thought away (of course you have to know about them first), and I express my thanks immediately. He will call for me when it's time. We both laugh: Time's a bit of a joke here.

Now some of you will no doubt be asking why a French music teacher and not an American? How did that come about? Well, quite simply, really. Gerard was over here (astral America, that is) for a Charles Ives performance (quite the spectacle, too: two orchestras and a marching band) and we met. As simple as that. We got talking about Satie and the rest you can imagine.

Anyway, the music's perked me up, too much for the lower astral, we'll have to get back to that later. Now I've got more of a mind to take you to one of the temples of wisdom that are dotted around the spheres. There are many types of these structures, and each one is keyed to the level of enlightenment enjoyed by the local inhabitants. Architecturally they come in all shapes and forms, from very ancient to very modern.

There are lectures, study groups, libraries, and gardens for contemplation. And they are all, as you say on Earth, open to the public. My current favorite is your basic Grecian, all marble colonnades with shafts of sunlight and interior courtyards with gardens designed from many traditions.

Now I know from reading over many shoulders on Earth that NDE literature has made these temples, and the teachers within them, familiar figures to many of you. Now you may see how it looks from here.

Hanging Around the Temples of Wisdom

In the one we're about to visit, I do occasional stints as the wise old man with his robe, beard, and stick, sunning himself by the melodious fountains of the salubrious inner courtyard. Sometimes I show up as a modern radical feminist with spiky hair and a T-shirt which says, "Make Up Your Own Mind," but today I fancy the Aristotle mode.

As I only appear from time to time, word gets around in my absence about my devastating insight, and the more conventional souls who are beginning to tire of the astral's endless holiday come around with their well-considered theories and await my eventual appearance.

I approach from a side entrance and slip unannounced into my regular position, the bench under the rose arbor adjacent to the fountain. On this occasion there seem to be five who have chosen to believe the myth of my omniscience rather than avail themselves of the services of the temple's other teachers, several of whom were attending to the floral displays attired as gardeners and the rest frolicking in the pool disguised as noisy children.

The group slows its chatter and smiles respectfully. The first approaches gingerly and I gesture for him to sit. After a long but gracious preamble, where the tidy attitudes of a former bureaucrat mingled and merged with the questing spirit of a teenage metaphysician and a soul who would soon be ready to reincarnate, came the big question.

What purpose did the world wars of the twentieth century serve? What on earth was the point of all that suffering? Surely the desired result could have been achieved with a greater economy of means.

It was not the first time I'd been asked this question and it would surely not be the last. Most are overwhelmed by the seeming immensity of the problem and are shocked by my succinct and cheery answer. In other hands they might be pointed towards the oppressive ideologies of communism, fascism, imperialism, or anti-Semitism, or perhaps the all-encompassing evil of vengeance.

But this serious soul seemed quite accepting when I said that the enslavement to the gods of nationalism had to be completely shattered for mankind to move on to the next stage of development, which is, of course, planetary consciousness.

He nodded as sagely as he dared, given what I could feel of his family's tragic disfigurement and his brother's lifelong antinuclear crusade, which I could sense had finally impinged on a self-satisfied bourgeois consciousness.

I pointed to the European Union as one of the first successful flowerings of the new internationalism, which, as an American, he had perhaps overlooked. Suddenly affronted, he pointed to Israel and Yugoslavia.

Isolated pockets of evolutionary laggards soon to be cleared up, I assured him, pointing out how influenced by national pride he still was, despite having only two American incarnations, the rest being evenly distributed around the globe. Suppressing shock, he stood up and thanked me for my time. I nodded.

A lady quickly took his place. Eagerness danced in her sparkling eyes. I had a feeling this one would be quick. Her former husband from Earth, now recently arrived, wanted to continue their relationship under one roof, and several members of her family thought it was an excellent idea, since she was so weak-willed and indecisive. She wanted to know, was she free to follow her heart, which urged independence, and would it create this bad karma she'd been hearing about?

I placed my hand on hers and smiled reassuringly. "Do what the heck you like and tell him to leave you be. Forget those aunties, move to another community and study the arts you so desire. Karma, my dear, is merely the results of your actions, and since all actions have results, you cannot avoid karma no matter what you do."

She looked stunned but pleased. I kissed her on the forehead and said, "Just grin and bear it." She leapt for joy like an amateur ballerina and quickly disappeared from sight.

The next one up was laughing and applauding. She seated herself accordingly. "I hear you're very wise."

I chuckled and stroked the old beard. "It's a heck of a reputation to live up to. And if the truth be told, it's mostly just an act. I'm really as thick as two planks. Don't know up from down or right from wrong. Typical bloody mystic, thinks everything's wonderful, all roads lead to the same place, etc., etc."

With this in her ear she shrieked joyously and then gave me a big bear hug. "That's just what I needed to hear, thank you!"

And off she went to whistle a merrier tune. I was beginning to feel like Santa Claus, but the next fellow up soon changed that. His first words were, in fact, screechingly funny, but this bountiful beard covers many a grin.

"Unaccustomed as I am to such levity, I shall proceed with my query, which I trust you will be able to answer."

"I shall do my very best, sir."

I had the notion he had been an antique dealer from somewhere in small town New England who rather worshiped the founding fathers. I thought, perhaps cynically, this'll be about religious freedom or the future of democracy.

I was wrong. He asked if progress were possible in a culture as corrupted as America. He assured me he'd given the matter much thought since he'd passed but had succeeded only in making himself gloomy.

It was all too easy to suspect a melancholy disposition at war with itself, so I skipped the elementary psychology and went straight for my answer. "Americans are like children reeling in horror as they realize Daddy's doing a few underhanded deals and bonking his brother's wife on the weekends. When they grow up they will see that all empires are created on the backs of deluded slaves and soldiers, from Atlantis and Egypt to France, Britain, and the United States. It's the way of the physical plane and the young ambitious souls who best adapt to its evolutionary schedule. Corruption is endemic to any such enterprise. As war is diplomacy under another name, corruption is business with a bigger profit margin. But it can still fund colleges, hospitals, and operas."

He looked, dare I say it, mildly impressed. If he'd been possessed of a beard I'm sure he would have stroked it thoughtfully. I should've offered him mine, but I didn't think of it till later. He thanked me for a stimulating reply but suggested I had avoided the question "is progress possible under such conditions?"

I replied, "The rise and fall of empires is a cyclical business whose amplitude and frequency are not worth tampering with, as it only leads to ever more subtle forms of addiction. But the individual soul can rise above such swirling tides to assume enlightenment as a birthright. Only then is he free of culture and its props. And that is the only real progress I know of."

He promised to consider my words carefully and return. Debating-team potential there, I thought.

The last fellow sat down promptly and, without any hint or invitation, launched into his problem. "I'm sick of the church. The rituals are pointless and the dogmas too dopey to even bother denying any more. I'm tired of looking for God. If he's not in the afterlife, where the hell is he?"

I sensed the elusive Zen master trip would suit this guy to a T, so I stared him in the eye, uttering as blankly as possible, "Love thy neighbor as thyself."

He did not seem pleased. I waved him away. I knew he'd be back.

As there was no one else in the immediate vicinity, I thought I'd take my leave. Normally, I stroll out slowly so that my admirers can easily vent their appreciation, but I was more in the mood to make a quick switch, so I thought myself back up to my own garden, where I reclined against my favorite willow and made a pretense of unwinding.

In a few of what you would think of as moments, I slipped into a purposeless meditative state and found myself floating in what I like to call "lilacland." Actually it's lilac shading into violet with ribbons of burnt umber and dusty jade wafting through, with a very restful, musical twittering all around. A delightfully formless space, it exists to shepherd its few inhabitants through an occasional thought-free bliss. A bit of an astral bath really, but, as you say down there, way better.

I've been here many times. It's my oasis of charm in a life of affectionate clutter. I don't recall how I first got here or where exactly it is. Maybe I made it behind my own back, who knows. All I can tell you is it's marvelously refreshing.

After some timeless time here I feel a twinge: Gordon's coming for a visit. That means he must be asleep in nighttime Canada. I return, somewhat reluctantly, to the willow, our usual meeting place.

Gordon, the "Author"

Perhaps now is as good an occasion as any to mention that the entire contents of this work constitute not much more than a few "days" of my life here in spirit. Not that we bother with "time" here, but when we are involved with Earth-plane activities, as I am in this project with Gordon, we notice, among other things, the frequency of OBE projectors, and that reminds us of the day and night rhythms you are subject to.

Gordon parts some overhanging branches, winks at me, and seats himself on the grass I know he recalls as unbelievably soft. And although his Earthly self sees this as a very special and sacred space, to his astral self it is as familiar and comfortable as an old shoe. He gazes at the garden and sighs, "Why can I never recall just how splendidly beautiful it is here? Tomorrow, I'll just have this vague memory of a garden and some kind of amusing conversation."

I tell him not to feel so bad. At least he remembers something and can patch together the rest from intuition and my thought projections. When I was alive on Earth the last time I had practically no astral consciousness at all. A few scattered flying dreams and that was about it.

That old Henry really had feet of clay. And it is funny to think of him now because I do feel quite distanced from him. I try to explain to Gordon what that feels like. The best comparison I can come up with is movies. He's like a hero I loved in my youth, whose dashing exploits I totally identified with but who now looks a little shopworn, a bit passé, somewhat out of date, and actually downright embarrassing from time to time. Still you have to forgive your former selves just as you must forgive, as the prayer says, those who trespass against you. Forgiveness is, after all, the ultimate breaker of karmic binds. Forgive them, as He said, for they know not what they do.

Gordon says, "Don't ruin it by getting all religious. I thought we were moving beyond spiritualism with this."

"Just teasing," I grin. Gordon's got some heavy baggage from unresolved past-life conflicts with the church and its bureaucracies, and he's not overkeen to deal with them. "Still clinging to your favorite resentments, Gordo?"

He mugs a complacent smile. Why don't I escort him to that level where all incarnations can be viewed simultaneously, as I have previously hinted at on several occasions? He's got me there. I've only glimpsed it myself, and I'm not entirely sure I have the nerve to go back. Not to mention my doubts as to whether an incarnate like Gordon could cope with the intensity. I tell him I'll have to take advice on it. Which is, despite his smirk, quite true. Even I have an advisor. Meanwhile there's a disaster team we could help out for awhile. Big floods in Central America.

I got the call as we were chatting. It was like a brief, high-pitched tone in the forehead in case you're interested. It signals to all interested parties: a natural disaster in progress.

As there are always those who wish to be of service in such situations, there are several teams who circle the globe constantly looking for trouble, as it were. Their numbers are made up of a rotating population of astral- and physical-plane dwellers who are specializing in what you might call anguish and terror management.

I introduced Gordon to this type of work at his request. Basically, he read about it somewhere and his interest was piqued. Like many aspirants, he said to himself: Hey, I can do that. But as the emotional pitch is significantly higher in these mass cases, it takes a great deal more equilibrium on the part of the rescuer, much more than is required in individual cases.

Gordon was more than a little overwhelmed on his first couple of tries. I told him to remain mentally focused but emotionally detached, rather as if he were on the verge of winning a very important chess game. This sounds good in theory, and aspirants always nod assertively, but when they are confronted with a tidal wave of burnt, maimed, or dismembered bodies and the putrid odors of terror, it's another story.

We flew over Central America looking for devastation. It was not hard to find. The storm had cut a rather large swath through several countries. The glow of helpers dotted the landscape. We settled on a flooded area that seemed particularly needy.

Gordon spied an old car sinking slowly in muddy floodwaters. He was right: A small family had been living in it. I could see a devastated village just downstream and wondered how many bodies were hidden by the muddy water.

He zipped into the car to check things out. I stood by, ready to help. An OBE's energy is that much closer to the Earth vibration and thus more easily recognizable to the recently dead.

He quickly discovered mother and child huddled together in the back seat next to their corpses. The father was trying to squeeze himself out the window he'd just succeeded in opening. Sheer unmitigated terror had given him the superhuman strength he needed to swim to shore.

Gordon coaxed the mother and child out of the car but not much farther. The woman would not leave her husband: She dashed about frantically looking for traces, with Gordon trailing her, quite patiently, I was pleased to see.

Finding her exhausted man crawling through mud to some kind of safety, she hovered about him trying to help and, I suspect, imploring him to come with her. Of course he could not hear her, and she could not understand why. Gordon wisely allowed her pathetic remonstrations to continue for some moments until she exhausted herself and collapsed beside her still-breathing mate.

I could see Gordon was finding the accumulating anguish progressively more unbearable, and although he well knew joining her in wailing would accomplish nothing, he could feel himself slipping. I stood close behind, reinforcing his sense of purpose.

He bent down close to her face and tried to speak kindly to her. His thought was to pluck her and the child she clutched from the scene of devastation, but I think he could see how slim his chances were. The woman could not bring herself to believe anything: the flood, her death, Gordon's appearance. She clung to her child and whimpered.

I told Gordon to stand back and went into my best impersonation of a radiant angel in the Catholic tradition. The woman was immediately affected and took me to be some kind of patron saint of lost travelers. I could not stop her from groveling at my feet, but after a few moments of the necessary debasement I managed to haul her up and get her to place an arm around my shoulder. As we lifted off for the nearest reception center, I motioned to Gordon to watch over the husband's body.

This he apparently did, as he was still in place after I dropped mother and child off at one of the tropical paradises being used for this operation, which I could see at a glance was a major one. I guessed at perhaps five times the magnitude of the Iranian earthquake of a few months before.

Before allowing me to depart, the woman begged me to save her husband. Calling her "child," which I sensed would be most effective, I counseled her to pray for the safe delivery of her mate. This seemed to mollify her and she allowed me to depart.

I found Gordon with the injured and grieving man, and I could see he was slipping. The thought had occurred to him that he actually wanted the man to die so that the family might be reunited, and he felt somehow guilty for it. His subsidence into guilt was fashioning a vibratory entry for the man's anguish and I told him if he didn't stop he would soon be in a worse state than his charge.

He asked if I would mind if he returned to my garden. He was sure he could no longer cope. I gave him a quick hug and off he went. I imagine he spent some quality time under the willow tree, recovering his balance before returning to the sleep of the living, for I became so busy with rescues that I did not return myself for quite some time.

The injured man, though close to death, was not quite there, and I left to look for riper possibilities. And although there were plenty of rescuers whizzing about, it did not take long to uncover a series of those dazed refugees recently expelled from the confinement of the corpse.

Most of them seemed to maintain a Catholic mindset, so as long as I looked appropriately saintly, things went quite smoothly. Only a couple showed the residue of mental torment that distinguishes the self-judged soul, convinced he is not good enough for God. Much joyful reunioning at the reception center later, I took my leave.

The Tragic Sensibility

✗ Entire ch.

The subject matter of the last chapter brings up some points that I've been intending to get around to for some time, ones that Gordon will no doubt remind me of on his next visit, should I overlook them now.

First, let me deal with what I call the "tragic sensibility." Those of you who read this work, and perhaps others like it, and feel energized and empowered by its revelations of eternal life should not be shocked if, on trying to spread the word, you encounter a high degree of skepticism.

As far as I can make out, from my current vantage point outside the flow of the historical enterprise, since at least the rise of scientific materialism and the consequent collapse of religious certainties, the tragic *c. 1650* sensibility is all that many people have left to hold onto.

The feelings of pity and compassion it arouses allow humans to feel good about themselves in a world seemingly gone mad.

When you come along and tell them that transition is a breeze and the afterlife more fun than they could ever imagine, it kinda knocks the wind outta their tragic sails and leaves them without a game plan for the trip. After all, what would life on Earth be without that struggle to keep one's head above water, both physically and spiritually?

The idea that suffering is created and sustained by human ignorance and would not exist without that ignorance to support it is a cross too heavy to bear for some folk. They would in fact rather bear the lesser cross of suffering because they're addicted to the way it makes them feel worthy.

In defense, these types will no doubt ask you to prove your assertions. I would advise you to refrain, as most skeptics do not care to be moved from their castles of sand but wish to stand in command of their shaky territory and mock all comers.

This brings me to some further reflections on Gordon. One of the interesting, and perhaps unique, aspects of this collaboration with him is that he feels very little, if any, compulsion for verification.

He says he feels no need, even feeling as he does, at the bottom of the well of the physical plane peeking up at the light of the astral, to prove anything to anyone. He says he has eliminated doubt from not only his vocabulary but also his consciousness.

Many OBE artists still feel the need to accumulate evidence of their experience that will satisfy the skeptic—out there in the world, but mostly within themselves.

Gordon says he wants to be an example for the future man, who, he is assured, will ascend from the exercise of the intellect to the exercise of the intuition, which will allow knowledge to flourish without the shadow of doubt. Convinced that the age of reason is at an end, he rather reiterates my position when he says that evidence does not defeat skepticism, but only inflates the desire to stiffen opposition.

Recalling Gordon's unfulfilled (as yet) request to experience that level of consciousness where all one's incarnations appear simultaneously brings me to this theme I have called "Beyond Heaven."

Just as on Earth a relatively small percentage of souls are courageous enough to leave the consensus reality of cities and villages to explore the rarified air of high mountain passes, so too in spirit only a few adventurous souls will quit the various consensus realities of the Heaven worlds to explore the high-energy states beyond.

Their Heavens, after all, are paradises of personal and cultural fulfillment, and only a few tire of such terminal bliss. The tales of the formless but sentient systems that lie beyond often fail to charm the conventional soul, who sees no point in what appears to be a renouncing of personality in favor of something more akin to being a teardrop in the ocean. But for the adventurous at heart, the ecstasy one receives in return for even temporarily renouncing the personality is more than worth the effort.

The transcendentally sublime can be hard to explain to those who feel they've already achieved the enchanting paradise of the upper astral or lower mental. Only a very few hardy souls wish to understand how being exists beyond energy.

Humans lolling in the splendid landscapes of Heaven will not hear of a further bliss where prophets have no positions, saviors no separate place, and societies, no matter how ideal, no significance.

Merging with the light retains little luster for their identity-bound selves. The proud achievements of community and culture constantly call them home. And while these are indeed wonderful accomplishments, they must be renounced in order to move on.

Creation of Reality on all Levels.

The oneness of Advaita?

Case Histories

As something of a guardian spirit, I come in contact with many types of souls in a variety of interesting circumstances. In this chapter I would like to outline a few of these case histories. The people involved are not my sole responsibility, but as someone with certain, shall we say, specialties, I pull people into my orbit who need a certain type of boost.

First up is the type of soul who sees the growth involved in a certain type of suffering as desirable and even glamorous. I call it the "crucifixion mentality" and am not always rewarded for my humor. There are those who take this sort of stuff very seriously, inspired as it is by that revered example at the eastern end of the Mediterranean some time back.

It is not unlike what my sister, Ann, hopes to achieve in the crib death she's now planning, but with a much larger quotient of pain. Of course, out here in spirit, pain is all too easy to scoff at. It's a different story down there stuck in agony and contempt.

And here would be as good a place as any to mention that sometimes the plans and advice of guides do not pan out quite the way we'd envisioned. You can set things up as neatly as possible, taking all the possible variations into account and using all your knowledge of psyches under stress, and still all you can do is hope for the best. Even here.

A recent example: This soul had been a bit lazy for several incarnations, settling for selfishness and the easy way out over and over again. Convinced by his counselors to make an exemplary effort, he hit upon the "crucifixion mentality" as a solution.

This involved volunteering to help tame another in that seemingly endless line of control-nut sadists. After all, every butcher needs his sacrificial lambs. He agreed to be born as the third child to an omnivorous ogre and his timid spouse.

There was some slight karmic link between them, but not enough to qualify as a debt. It was more an act of service and forgiveness than anything. He'd brothered and befriended this demented soul a couple of times, including the life with the abusive drunken warrior father that had sparked it all. This time he knew it would be short and far from sweet, but he was so close to that mastery of illusion that accompanies unconditional love that he thought he'd go for it. And do not be surprised that this near mastery of illusion was followed by several lives of taking the easy way out; it often happens that a soul near the finish line falls into dawdling.

For ten months he was starved, beaten, and generally raked over the coals while the terrified mother looked on and made excuses to the authorities. The constant pain and overwhelming sense of abandonment pushed him out of the body much more even than is normal for babies, and in this expanded state he tried to mirror the light of love into the home. And although he succeeded in dissipating some of the manic thrust of the demonic spirits assisting in stoking this domestic inferno, he could not break down the core of depravity.

Finally dropped on his head, the spine snapped, and away he went up through the levels to that ocean of bliss where form is but a performance put on for the fun of it.

For the purposes of this narrative I dropped in on the trial of the two degenerates. It was the usual ritual of sluggish grief and righteous vengeance, that vigorous clamor for even more cruelty that is the lot of those who remain confined by fear. The mob scene outside the courthouse was something to behold. From this level the aggrieved emotions manifest as blood-red and bile-green explosions above the distorted faces.

Of the many shocked passers-by however, a couple were committed Christians, and their silent prayers provided some psychic space for the spirits above to send some blessings of peace, so that if only one or two overcame their rage and wondered later if perhaps there was a meaning in it all, then at least a little something was stirred into the pot of ignorance and fear.

There are, of course, sunnier sides to this ongoing energy conversion. One soul I visit with from time to time has elevated her obsessions with pain and suffering this time around to something on the level of "art form" or "therapy."

She's a high-priced, inner-city dominatrix. Men obsessed with the pursuit and control of power, finding themselves mysteriously frustrated in the exercise of their desires, come to her for the subjugation and punishment which alone will give them a release.

She makes no bones about her enjoyment of these sessions, which give her the freedom to control and inflict. "Everyone's needs are being met," she tells me when out of body, as she was this morning (her time, just after the flood retrievals) in something she might vaguely recall as a pleasant dream.

I pointed out that the behavior patterns are still obsessive and the souls far from realizing their true nature. "Ah yes," she says, gleaming, "but I'm edging them towards it, and the relationships I develop with my long-term clients are often more real and more devoted than my actual friends and family."

She tells me she knows it's no more than the divine play of energies on the physical plane, and just the sort of play she's particularly happy with, and besides, a girl has to earn a living, don't you know.

I warn her about not believing all she reads in those best-selling new-age books, and we part laughing. That is, she disappears mid-laugh, probably to answer one of nature's calls, and I continue to chuckle, wondering who, if anyone, will show up next.

Since it's morning in most of the Americas I cater to, probably no one. Wanda, due to the nature of her business and personal inclinations, usually goes to bed just before dawn, which brings her my way sometime after most of my regulars who keep more conventional hours.

It was her appearance and conversation, however, that prompted me to scour the archives for some more case histories, not all of which are contemporaneous with the real-time exposition of this work, but are still recent and relevant.

Now what about Glenn and Helen, over in that cabin in the woods not far from here? Now there's a real Romeo and Juliet archetype for you. Gassed themselves in Glenn's father's car a few months back. Only fifteen the two of them, and as you can imagine, mad for each other.

Filled with love and devotion to their mutual amour rather than anger and resentment at the families that contrived to keep them apart, they were floated up and out of that car and drifted to the idyllic retreat in the woods they'd often fantasized about in their furtive meetings after school.

Guided by spirits they had no inclination to see, they found the cabin as if by magic and settled there immediately to play house and garden. A dream come true, they doted on each other like a couple happily married for decades. Quite self-sufficient, they were left to their own devices until the time seemed right for a friendly intervention.

Their guides assured me they had not been bothered by the pull of their funerals, such was their mutual admiration. Whether stiffened with pride or abject with remorse, perhaps both, the parents had suffered in uncommunicative silence. Such is the karma of unstinting pride and ambition.

This is my second visit. They entertain me with tea and cookies, and we sit in the garden admiring the birds. Some ramblers pass by and wave. Glenn says they are regulars and Helen giggles at some private joke. I ask all the usual questions one produces for new neighbors: Were they happy with the house? Were they settling in? Did they need any help with anything?

Helen pipes up, "Like we really are dead, eh?"

I nod and smile. "You bet, Helen. There's no escaping it. How does it feel?"

She giggles. "It's awesome, Henry, just absolutely the best."

Glenn adds, "I feel as light as a feather."

"That's because you are as light as a feather."

"You're kidding right?"

"No, sir, it's all been measured ages ago." I go on to explain about the lack of gravity, or, more correctly, the abundance of it on the physical plane, and how the tons per square inch make you so leaden, but it seems to slip by them. As a clincher I ask if they've tried flying yet. Obviously not. I illustrate with a modest upward drift and wave from on high. Glenn says he'll try it, but I'll have to tell him how.

"Just imagine," is my answer.

"Just imagine what?"

"That you're floating."

And he does. And not bad for a first timer. Fairly steady, no sudden reversals, as is often the case. I encourage him to try a couple of swoops across the garden, but Helen calls, "Come and get me first!"

Settling back down beside her and grabbing her hand, he confidently pulls her up. It was just a little tug really, just enough to convince her, and soon they were floating around above the garden in a fit of giggles. Their childish joy is something to behold, even for an old hand like me.

Glenn's "Man, are we ever dead now!" seems to sum it all up. Eventually I couldn't resist joining them and showing off a few tricky maneuvers. Out here everyone's a bit of a gymnast, I told them. And it's true: Only the stiffest and most formal of souls can resist the urge to fly once they're shown the ropes.

Later they show me around the cabin, which, even with its basic furnishings, they are extremely proud of, despite Helen's misgivings about the curtains. They just woke up in it one day, they tell me. How they got there from Glenn's father's car is anyone's guess. I smile and tell them about God working in mysterious ways and that they needn't have any curtains at all if they don't want them. Helen is cheered, but Glenn doesn't seem to care.

Helen is wondering about food in the pantry: No matter how much they eat there always seems to be more. I told them it was imagination at work again. As long as they wanted food it would be there. Glenn asks about toilets, where were they? Nowhere I say, unless you want to make one. That brings us back to thought forms, a concept that quite went over their heads the first time I mentioned it and doesn't seem to ring too many more bells this time either.

I explain that the food is imaginary and will slowly disintegrate when they stop thinking about it. Disintegrate into what, Glenn wants to know. Well, nothing. Or particles so small they might as well be nothing.

Well, what about babies, Helen asked; they'd been fucking like mad since they got here and still no signs. I was sorry, but there was no baby-making here. That was only on Earth. Helen looks profoundly disappointed. But, I continue cheerfully, you can always adopt, there are plenty of dead babies that need caring for here. I can take them to just such an astral plane orphanage when they feel ready. Glenn says they will need to discuss that privately.

I float up to the treetops and wave goodbye. They look stunned. I call, "If you need something, just give me a call."

Glenn shouts, "How? There's no phones."

"Just imagine me and I'll be there."

They laugh a little nervously and I am gone. I like a dramatic exit once in a while.

Entrances too. Just walk in a door somewhere, talking.

This time it's Bob and Carole's rest home. Bob's in his favorite sitting room, reading Proust in the original, something he never had time for on Earth, and something he just can't get enough of here. I've long since given up teasing him about it. After all he lives with a woman who reads Ibsen in Norwegian, so what chance do I have?

I peek in, nod, and head up to Kelly's room, which is, by the way, decorated with pictures of Mel Gibson and Tom Cruise. I met her here a while back, just after her death in a stolen car, the joyride of her life, she informed me proudly, even though it killed her. "I always knew I was immortal," she bragged on that first meeting. Kids these days, I tell ya.

Today she informs me of her first visit to her upcoming fetus. She describes it as a concentrated ball of light floating in an ocean of maroon. It belongs, apparently, to her recently married elder sister, Marian. It will be great, she says, it will give her the chance to show some joy and love to her former mother Gillian, who was still grieving over her death. Mother or grandmother, what difference does it make?

And she's willing to come clean and admit that she was a typical teen rebel, thinking only of herself and causing Gillian and her stepdad, Derek, untold worry with her wild impetuous behavior.

And although I earlier advised her to delay her reentry into the physical, fearing a pointless repetition of behavior patterns, others have convinced her the risk is worth it. She assures me she is committed to doing it right this time and assures me she will faithfully attend classes in incarnate recall.

This will, if it works, make her one of those wise and wonderful three-year-olds who chatter about their former lives and send shivers down everyone's spine with profound utterances at the breakfast table.

I would have preferred her to chill out here a little longer, and I tell her so, but it seems wiser heads than mine will prevail. I ask if she's consulted her sister about this. Apparently not, but she is fully intending to do so the next time she's asleep. Meanwhile she's got a class to go to. She bustles about significantly.

I bid her farewell and walk downstairs to see Carole, who has only just returned from a talk by the great Ibsen himself, which she proudly tells me she flew over to the astral version of Norway for. It only takes a few moments longer than thinking yourself there, but those endeared of flying, as Carole is, find it ever so much fun.

She asks how I'm doing and laughs when I say splendid. She thinks I'm a real character. I always say I'm a real seventeen characters and that just makes her laugh more. Bob's having wine with his Proust, perhaps we should join him and discuss the role of literature in the evolution of culture.

Well, I say, grinning, perhaps I can spare a few moments. Your mother and son duo are off at a concert, she winks, you're safe. We barge in on Bob, who seems as relaxed as ever. Carole sits on his lap and chatters away in Norwegian. Chuckling, I move to fetch the wine.

Instead of the role of literature in culture, we fall to discussing my project with Gordon. Although I doubt he remembers, they have met on a few occasions. Carole specifically recalls a discussion she had with him, decades ago Earth time, when he was feeling depressed and suicidal over a relationship breakup.

She claims she talked him out of it, suicide that is. She still recalls him saying that relationship problems were by far the biggest Earthbound burden for him. Bob can't forget a love affair that ended badly before he met Carole; it still shakes him to think of how self destructive he became, boozing and getting into fights.

"I was your little rescue angel, wasn't I?"

"You sure were, sweetheart. And I wouldn't mind betting you've done much the same in other lives."

"We really should check that out sometime."

I'd chastise them for being spiritually lazy if I weren't so bad myself, not to mention the fact that Gordon will read this and be appalled. You mean my spirit guide doesn't know all his past lives? Maybe he'll trade me in for a new model, one that can do enlightenment at 8.6.

Bob suggests I do some man-on-the-street interviews at one of the large reception centers so readers can get a glimpse of the variety of possible reactions to transition. Off the top of the head stuff, first impressions.

It sounds like a good idea to me, so after some more chit-chat I disappear, only to reappear at the reception center on the shores of Lake Ontario (astral version).

A number of souls are out on the sandy beach relaxing. Some children splash about, some in the water, some on it. That's another little thing you can do here. It's easy once someone shows you how. As I said to Glenn, it's mainly a case of "just imagine."

I come across two women first. After greeting them I sit down and explain my purpose. The seemingly younger of the two was actually the mother on Earth, but has been here two years. The genetic daughter, looking older, just passed two days ago and is having her first stroll about. A cancer victim, she can't believe how easy it was. A year of suffering gone in a flash. It was like carrying a really heavy bucket for ages and then realizing you could just drop it, she says. And it's great to be back with dear old mum, even though she had to leave her boys behind to do it. But they're old enough to look after themselves now, and if they're not they'll sure as hell have to learn in a hurry. This, as you might guess, is delivered with a laugh shared by the mother.

Thanking them, I move on. Next is an older man with a much younger woman, who turns out to be his first wife, dead twenty-odd years and, of course, loving every minute of it. She's wearing a rather old-fashioned dress, I think to remind him of when they were both young. He's still in the clothes he died in, which, since it's summer down there, is shorts, sandals, and short-sleeved checked shirt.

He was walking the dog when this stolen truck spun out, whipping around a corner at about 120 he reckons. Bloody dog wasn't touched, he says, smirking, never liked it anyway. Was the wife's apparently. Second wife that is. And what a bitch she was. Couldn't stand her, couldn't afford to live without her. Nightmare on wheels. But now he's with his Jessie again, and God she's even better than he remembers. Throws his arms around her, gives her a big kiss.

He looks like her dad but tells me he understands about this getting younger day by day. Suits him, never liked being old anyway. Jessie says she's just glad to be together again. She's watched over him all this time and has a house all ready, and as soon as he gets out of the hotel she'll be taking him there.

I bid them adieu and walk on. I come across two children, a boy and a girl about five or six, making shapes in the sand. I ask them how it's going. They stop their game and look at me. I sense a little discomfort and sit down beside them.

I tell them I'm going around the beach asking people how they got here. The girl, as cute as Shirley Temple with her curly locks tells me they're from Detroit and were all killed in a carjacking. At least she and her brother and father were killed right away. But they had to follow the ambulance to the hospital to get their mother, who died in emergency. That's their mum and dad over there.

I turn to look at what would pass for a sunbathing couple anywhere on the continent. The man gets up on one elbow. "That's right, we're all dead and can't hardly believe it."

The mother sits up and smiles. "If you ask me, it's the best thing we ever did as a family. If it wasn't for the grandparents sulking it'd be just perfect."

The father gives her a little shove. "Nonsense. If your mother was here you'd be dying to get away."

I ask how long they'd been here.

"Probably about a week, we're not sure," the father says.

"The funeral was about three days ago," continued the mother, "we think."

I laugh and thank them for their time.

"What time?" laughs the father. "If you find any, come back and tell me, will you?"

I come across two teenage girls stretched out on towels. One is lying on her stomach reading a magazine and the other is sitting cross-legged, carefully painting her fingernails blue. They seem oblivious to my presence.

"Do ya wanna catch that fashion show?"

"Yeah, why not . . . might be fun."

I excuse the interruption and tell them my purpose. The reader looks up at me and calmly announces, "Meningitis." The cosmetician copies her tone with "Teenage sex trade worker murdered by crazy fucker. And there's two more over there." She nods toward two others stretched out and seemingly asleep.

My "How long?" is answered with "Month, maybe."

"Miss your folks?"

"You gotta be kidding, mister. It's fuckin' great to get away. You ever frozen your ass on the sidewalk tryin' to turn tricks?" She looked me over. "Nah, didn't think so. Shelley here's my best friend and I ain't known her a month."

I thank them for their contribution and move on.

Seeing a chubby middle-aged man about to go for a swim, I walk over to join him.

"Great resort, huh? I could hardly believe my luck when I got here." He offers me his hand. "Bernie Andrews, Acuras and Lexus. Salesman of the month April, May, and June. Really pure smack in July. Blew the old ticker to bits. How about you?"

He was amazed to find out I'd been dead since sixty-three. Only born in fifty-three himself. We reach the water's edge. He asks me what I've been doing all this time. Like how long can you be on vacation.

I mention some of the opportunities that will open up as he relaxes into his new life. Having a new house seems to be about the only thing that appeals to him right now. He admits he's a bit lonely and not really adjusted but seems cheered by the observation that his wife is now tooting so much coke with her boyfriend it can't be much longer till she gets here herself.

I warn him that she may only want to hang around cokeheads even after she's dead. He says yeah, he spent a while doing that himself, glomming onto his dealer, trying to get a hit. Bastard wouldn't give him any, he laughs. Fortunately he was only a weekend user and was able to lick the habit and come here.

He waddles into the water and I wave to him as he swims away looking very pleased with himself. A little revelation of character, you might be saying to yourself, and you would be right. The astral is as good for that as the physical. People watchers have lots of fun here.

On the lawn leading up to one of the many residences dotted about the lakeshore, I come across a group of seniors playing bridge. Died in a nursing home fire. Just as well too. Place was a firetrap and the nurses thieving psychos. Families leave you there to rot, waiting to divvy up the goodies. Ed, Stan, Joyce, and Geeta. If you can imagine the last five sentences uttered in a clockwise fashion you've just about got it.

As I stroll away, Joyce calls, "And you can tell them the food is fabulous here!"

I wave and nod. I'm good at that.

The place looks like a typical lakeside resort. That may sound dull and unimaginative, but it's intended to make the recently deceased feel right at home. There's about half a dozen of them stretched out along the shore, catering to different social classes and tastes.

[Not that there are any enforced class distinctions here. People can wander anywhere they choose, as long as they keep within their vibrational "comfort zone," as it were. To simplify, let me say that horizontal movement is open to all, but vertical is for those ready to transcend their self-imposed limitations.]

Here's some people in the lobby all set to play tennis. Mixed doubles by the look of things. I introduce myself and my mission. They all laugh. They all died in a twenty-two-car pileup in morning fog along the interstate. Deborah and Steve were workmates and secret lovers. Wanda is Hank's sister-in-law, staying with him while she searched for a new job.

They've all left children and spouses behind but are trying to make the best of it. And it's so much fun here they all feel a bit guilty, leaving everyone else to struggle with the snow shoveling and mortgage payments. Their transitions were quite simple, as there were plenty of helping spirits hovering about the crash site.

Wanda insists on telling me this, saying, "Make sure this gets in the book, I want people to read this." While on Earth she'd gotten fascinated in reading about the NDE experience, especially one case where a young mother of three reported feeling such an overwhelming bliss when out of the body that she didn't, even for a moment, miss her three little children.

Well, she couldn't accept it when she read it, but she sure understands it now. She was killed outright in the collision and her first few moments dead were almost indescribably ecstatic. She says, "Say this: a bliss beyond compare, and I'm not the slightest bit religious."

[Of course, she laughs, she's an old hand now, dead at least a week, and yes, all this fun really is becoming quite humdrum, but what the heck, somebody's got to do it. And as her guide said, everyone gets here sooner or later, so why sweat it.]

Deborah and Steve tell me, in that eager sharing of sentences that couples have, that they've decided that this is what they secretly wanted, to be together, but they never thought they'd have to die to do it. Their spouses won't talk to them but are eagerly cashing in the life insurance policies. Their guides have assured them it's all very karmic, but they haven't had the nerve to check it all out yet. "Vacation time," they smile.

Hank had reached some kind of impasse in his life, really stuck for a new direction. Long divorced and quite distanced from his daughter, now on the West Coast with her mother, he'd gone around in circles for years, just making himself more and more miserable. And no, just in case we're wondering, he wasn't having an affair with Wanda.

In fact letting her stay while she looked for a new job was the first decent thing he'd done in years. Too busy feeling sorry for himself, he now thinks. They excuse themselves and wish me luck with my project. I thank them for their input and tell them my amanuensis on Earth will be fascinated with their stories.

I find the dining room: Some folks are still eating lunch. Looking around, I tune in on their various hungers. From peckish to voracious, the human family feeds.

Of course, at this early stage in their postmortem careers, regular meals seem indispensable, and they taste so good no one can imagine why anyone would want to give them up. They are told that as they settle in they will feel less and less need for such substantial nourishment, but they don't really believe it. They nod politely, not wishing to offend, but continue to dig in. And who am I to point the finger, I was just the same when I arrived.

In the midst of this happy feasting it occurs to me to take you on a quick ride up the astral elevator just for a contrast. From souls who are still attached to their food, I shall take you by souls who are still attached to their emotions; those who've shed the personal attachments and are learning to navigate those realms of sentient excitement; and then past souls who are still enmeshed in the endless creative versatility of thoughts; to those who, having mastered both emotion and thought, have shucked both body and identity and are content to merge with the ineffable.

I call it ineffable, for in the formless worlds verbal description achieves little but confusion, even for readers of relative sophistication. Suffice it to say that when a soul has left the astral and spent whatever mental capacity it has so far achieved in absorbing wave after wave of thought, it sees it has had its fill and knows that even creativity has its boundaries. *Beyond the belief structures?*

From there it is easy to slip into the formless. The attachment to shape and personality just melts. One knows that just being is the supreme pleasure, that light is its own reward. One is light surrounded by light, wearing the consciousness version of a grin. It could even be said that one is smiling in one's own home.

Limitlessness

Changing Levels within the Planes

Is easy for me because I know how. I know because I was taught by Jack, my golfing buddy spirit guide, some time after getting settled. I noticed that he was quite adept and asked if he would teach me, which he did with much joking and teasing.

It will not be hard for you to learn when you get here, as you most certainly will, especially if you have the inclination to expand beyond your level of comfort. Until that time, let me give you a sample.

You've already had a taste of the lowest levels, or at least some of them. Believe me, there's plenty more where they came from. For example, plenty of astral slums where the angry, embittered, tormented, and loveless roam, reaching out only to torment and be tormented. Of course, these are not slums of the merely poor, these are slums of the spirit, where, as often as not, the depraved rich reunite to regale each other in ghastly tatters.

For every physical North American city there are at least two, if not three, astral counterparts, catering to the various levels of spiritual attainment. Yes, three New Yorks, three San Franciscos, three Buffalos. It may sound almost too fantastic to be true, but trust me it's there.

There's no overestimating the size of the spirit world. It just goes on and on and on. Imagine walking across the continent and never getting sore feet or hungry or bored. That's what it's like touring the astral.

Let's take a look at low-level Buffalo. Not much different from low-level St. Louis or Chicago. Same faces, same character types, same attitudes. Kill or be killed. Dog eat dog. Yes, it prevails.

In the spectrum from mischievous to malicious, the tormentors and the tormented continue on their merry-go-round, knowing neither that they're dead nor that their reality is a composite of thought forms and expectations. After all, everything looks much the same as before and people act much the same.

A knife cannot kill, nor truly dismember, but it will frighten the ignorant and keep aggressors at bay. There is nothing to steal except thought forms, but they seem real enough when you snatch them. Look, there's something going on now: A fight has erupted outside a bar. Two groups of young black men, one with red bandannas, one with blue, going at it with the kind of tireless ferocity only attainable here on the astral.

Since they expect conditions to be the same as on Earth, bruises, broken limbs, and bleeding erupt within seconds. I don't think even one of them knows they are dead, so enraptured are they with the tides of their turf war. Doubtless there are stashes of crack and money to be won out of this.

Winners emerge and then escape. Let's walk over and see what's what. A wounded man, clutching a rag to his thought-form wound, leans over a fallen comrade, who he is sure is dying. My approach is not welcomed; I am seen to be interfering in a very private moment. My gestures of assistance are judged insincere and I am invited to immediately relocate.

I insist that I am a healer and can save them both. This offer is instantly examined for guile and scorn and, surprisingly, is then given space. As clothes (on this level) still make the man, I have taken care to appear white robed and savior-like. These dudes have never been churchgoers, but I suspect some religious imagery has crept in via television.

As I begin a classic hands-on healing, the sort of thing only seen on the physical plane in places like Brazil, I'm of two minds about whether to tell them they're dead. Ah, probably just confuse them if I told them now.

I tell the prone young gentleman to focus on the healing power of spirit. He tells me, in no uncertain terms, that the pain is too great. I stare rather forcefully into his eyes and ask if he wants to recover. He answers in the affirmative. I tell him to try.

Lo and behold, my subterfuge works. The blood stops, the ragged cuts smooth over and all is apparently well. After a repeat performance on his comrade, I quickly become the hero of the moment and am invited back inside for a drink. Backslaps and grins are the order of the moment. During a round of thought-form whiskies I am asked where I am from. Choosing my answer as a cad twirls his moustache, I announce that I'm from the land of the dead.

This garners a few chuckles. "How'd you git here, man?"

"I appear from time to time."

"And jist do yo' stuff?"

"You bet. And how did you get here?"

There follows an involved tale of gangsta rap, drug dealing, dance clubs, and crooked cops that seems to revolve around getting status in the ghetto and maintaining it. After numerous shoot-outs and drive-bys a number of the home boys found themselves here, in this hood with no cops. My miraculous healing has been momentarily forgotten.

Was I gonna teach them my mojo, this seems to be paramount in their minds. Plenty of pussy is to be pushed my way. In fact one gracious young lady is importuned to purvey an immediate sample. I politely decline her immediate services, suggesting a later and perhaps more luxurious assignation. She seems charmed.

I tell them my mojo is merely the power of thought, and that all they have to do is believe in themselves to make it work. Did I mean they could heal all their own wounds any time they wanted? Yes, that was indeed the case. Think the wound away, I continue, and away it goes. Just imagine yourself whole and healthy.

And how did this shit work, they wanted to know, after the clinking of glasses and laughter subside. It works because this is the land of thoughts. Their eyes momentarily narrow. This, I declare, holding up my shot glass, is a thought, these bottles are thoughts, this building is a thought. They're only here because you think they should be here.

"Man, yo' shittin' us."

"I most certainly am not, sir."

"Show us."

I hold out the palm of my right hand, stare at it with an unaccustomed degree of severity, and then look back at my two companions. I can see the young lady hovering behind them, intrigued. I ask if they were paying attention. They nod in unison.

The act of creation isn't nearly as easy on these denser lower planes as it is in the mid-astral where most of the dead reside and discover the power of thought for themselves, but it can be learned and utilized with the type of instruction given me by Jack. Firstly, you have to believe it's possible; and secondly, you must exert complete control over your thoughts. That is, no wavering. You must take the image and bring it carefully to life.

The best example you have on Earth right now is computerized animation. My creation of a three-inch man, complete with blue jogging suit and trendy trainers, looks much as it would in a Disney film. One moment there is nothing, the next he is there, smiling and waving as I intend him to be.

My companions are enthralled: One of them makes a grab for the figure, but I dematerialize him instantly.

Chuckling: "Not so fast, partner."

"Man, how'd you do that?"

"Thought, my friend, thought."

I pick up a glass from the bar and make it disappear. A few seconds later it reappears on the bar. I ask them what their preference is. Tequila is the answer. I imagine the glass with two ounces of the amber liquid and offer the result around.

The bartender, who a few moments earlier seemed to regard me as some kind of harmless crank who would soon be dispatched, now regards me warily, no doubt concerned that his supply of thought-form money will soon be drying up.

My new friends are, dare I say it, mighty impressed. I tell them all they have to do is believe and practice. With a polite au revoir I am on my way. As I make it to the door, the young lady previously assigned arrives by my side.

We stroll down the grimy and sullen street like a courting couple, her excited chatter telling me I am a cut above her usual companions. She makes it plain she has rooms in a house nearby. The neighborhood is your average urban decay gone astral.

You may wonder why anyone would choose an afterlife like this, but for many of the residents, ignorance precludes choice. The short period of lost consciousness that follows their violent death allows people to think they've somehow changed neighborhoods to one that's miraculously free of cops. The atmosphere is still gloomy and the surroundings decrepit, but as they don't expect any better their comfort zone is sustained.

The young lady leads me down an alleyway. She apologizes for the mess but it's the safest way to her place. I ask if she knows she's dead. She turns and presses herself against me. As her tongue probes my mouth, her breasts rub against my chest. Even someone as holy as I cannot mistake the sincerity of the invitation. And as usual the warm intensity of its rendering is offered up as evidence of its extreme lack of death.

I tell her with a grin that horniness is universal and eternal and that not even death can dampen its native enthusiasm. Does that mean I don't wanna fuck her, she pouts. Well not exactly. I want her to realize she's dead.

And get her shit together and go along with me, she continues, not missing a beat. Well, she'd do that, but there was plenty of time to get it on first, wasn't there? What was the big goddamn hurry? She rubs her crotch against my thigh. My reaction evinces the following: "You's jist like the dude from de Baptist church."

I know I am cornered; she's trapped me in her gaze. The dance of sin and redemption, a dance as illusory and ancient as the dream of life itself. In the lingo, I want to lay my trip on her as much as she wants to lay her trip on me. We're even.

Maybe I'll try a touch of chivalry. Standing back, I make an elaborate gesture out of raising and kissing her fingertips. Floating slowly upwards, I bid her farewell. She gazes after me, equal parts anger and amazement.

Again, at this level, with a density nearly that of the physical plane, flying is a rarity, unlike the mid- and upper-astral, where it is an everyday occurrence in everything from children's games to elaborate sports. There is, for example, an aerial version of synchronized swimming, which is, as you can imagine, a delight to behold.

Sub-Planes

As we move upwards to examine the next most interesting level, I should point out that there are many sub-planes between the so-called major ones. Basically they are there to cater to the almost (but not quite) infinite levels of consciousness held by the deceased.

For example, just above our last stop there is a level where souls are petty, mean-spirited, vindictive, and gossipy in a back-stabbing sort of way, but never quite criminal in the conventional sense. Most of them know they're dead but seem not to care, carrying on with their spiteful, resentful grouchiness. Of course, they wind up with the same nasty quarrelsome neighbors they had on Earth, as that is just what they deserve and will, in fact, keep, as long as they need to learn that lesson. To walk down a street in one of their towns is to know the scowl, the averted gaze, and the whispered suspicions.

Sometimes religion is the excuse, sometimes politics, sometimes race. And even, more recently, gender. For example, separatist lesbians did not exist as any sort of community on the astral when I arrived, but there are a few groups now, some radically politicized and some the victims of hard drugs and AIDS. Like all polarized groups, they are left alone to pursue their goals. There is never any concerted pressure to join what you might think of as "society at large," mostly because there is no society at large that can be said to share a common vision (other than maybe the sheer bliss of being dead), just a bewildering variety of what I have already called "communities of shared interests."

I found most of them to be disgruntled materialists, so of course they are as surprised as any to find themselves still alive and kicking. I suspect it was only their fierce love for one another that drew them this far across the veil. For spirituality I discovered they often turn to Wicca, that ancient worship of nature in all its spiritual guises, as purveyed to them by some wise old witches who understand the nature of their wounds.

You'll perhaps not be surprised to hear that I took the female form in order to penetrate their defenses. I called myself Cassandra and catered to their expectations by appearing in jeans, sweatshirt, and spiky dyed-blonde hair. A disguise that worked so well I had to rework it only slightly for use at the temple of wisdom for those occasions when I did not care to have my reputation precede me.

The next plane I fancy for a visit is one of the slightly less glamorous mid-astrals, which perfectly fits the bill for that type of soul who's always figured on an afterlife but is sure they've put in a less than spectacular performance and are not worthy of Heaven's glories . . . yet. For Catholics, of course, this has been conceptualized as Purgatory, but the soul state it represents covers all denominations.

The communities are small, drab towns plunked down in bleak prairie landscapes under ominous, cloudy skies which occasionally break for a burst of inspirational sunshine. Churches, libraries, and theatres are well attended, and the inhabitants are polite in a hopeful way, although their burdens of regret and self-criticism are all too obvious.

I want you to meet my friend Cliff who patrols these places evangel-izing. A one-man Christian ministry, Cliff is. He lives on the next level up in a reasonable facsimile of Christian Heaven. I love to tell him how it's really the Summerland of the Spiritualists being usurped by the very ones who denied it on Earth, but he usually refuses to be drawn into debate.

We'll probably find him at his favorite café, sipping a fruit juice and regaling some poor innocent with his tales of Heaven. Yes, there he is, just as I suspected.

He gestures grandly at the seat beside him and, as he orders juice and a cookie for me, offers to pay as long as I don't harangue him about karma and reincarnation. I laugh good-naturedly but make no promises.

I ask how things are in Heaven these days. He assures me they're perfect, as always. Why, just the other day Saint Paul came by to lay out his blessings.

Is he sure it was the original and not some stand-in from central casting? Absolutely not, the glow was unmistakable. Cliff goes on to recount the upscale glory of the occasion, the thousands of faithful in attendance, the massed choirs exultant with hosannas, and the almost careless promiscuity of sectarian blending. Episcopalians and Baptists shoulder to shoulder with Lutherans and Anglicans. Why, there were even some new agers there. This I get with a wink and a chuckle, as Cliff has me pegged as a new ager. I keep telling him I've been dead too long for that, but I don't think he believes me.

The hip thing in my day was Zen, as presented to America by Alan Watts. I can still recall the sentence that inspired me the most: "The immediate now, whatever its nature, is the goal and fulfillment of all living." Strange for a dyed-in-the-wool accountant you might be saying, and you would be right, were it not for my old rival of many rounds, Reid, who passed me Alan Watts's *This Is It* sometime in 1960, igniting some kind of flame that the tussle over Veronica was completely unable to douse. Remind me to thank him for that, will you?

Anyway, Cliff's only been over for a couple of years, caught in a rip-tide somewhere around Hawaii, and I guess my theological position sounds too bizarre to be anything but new age to him. And he's not the first dead Christian to keep mentioning Shirley MacLaine as if she were responsible for it all. I can see she's become some kind of symbol.

I remind him of something I mentioned in our last meeting: that on the next level beyond his, former Muslims and Christians live together in peace and even worship together. Now, for a man who lived believing only certain types of Christians went to Heaven, this is anathema. It's almost as outrageous as reincarnation. *against the fundamentalist dogma*

Anyway, we agree to disagree. I tell him about this project and why I'd like to include his activities. Like many Christians he's almost completely ignorant of the history of spiritualism, with its decades of glad tidings from the dead to the living, so the notion that his little tour of duty here might become known to some New Age book readers paralyzes him with a kind of impatient petulance I've seen before: He doesn't care to aid some cause he disapproves of, but you never know, I might be converted if he appears to meet me halfway.

Before we join him on his rounds, let me expand on a small but significant point. When I teased Cliff about the "original" Saint Paul, I was touching on a much debated point hereabouts. The historically revered figures of religion and culture, the people that everyone expects to see when they get to their version of Heaven, can be, and often are, played by "actors"—the originals having left their safe berth for another birth into space and time.

These actors, sometimes called "aspects," are all quite evolved and sincere beings who are in no way perpetrating any fraud but see themselves as providing a service for the millions who require the experience of adulation. They understand why humans need to be inspired, and they go about their tasks with humility and dedication.

But the souls who require such divine animation inevitably insist upon originality. Any mention of such duplications is considered derogatory and disrespectful. So, despite the live-and-let-live atmosphere of most planes, one learns to be discreet. The bottom line is that every belief system considers its prophets sacrosanct and will not stand for any meddling, although I must say they're all considerably more polite than they were on Earth.

I like to needle souls like Cliff because I know they all need a little shove towards their higher self, that pinnacle of their being that lies beyond all belief systems in the void of the unmanifest, and which, by appearing to not exist in any recognizable form, scares the living shit out of them, thus propelling them along a line of personalities promoting their culture as a corrective to fear.

Enough philosophizing.

Cliff asks, as we move off towards a house on the edge of town, how I propose to communicate this stuff to Earth with any degree of reliability, and then, as I formulate an answer I deem suitable to his level of understanding, he decides he doesn't really want to know after all.

You'll probably be wanting some description of the surroundings on this level. Well, rather dog-eared is the first phrase that comes to mind. Squat, drab bungalows that look as though they survived the depression, but only just. Trees and bushes just coming into leaf. Several passers-by staring at their feet. A kind of endless April suffusing the air. Cliff, of course, insists on being cheerful with everyone. After all, he's the bearer of glad tidings, so why shouldn't he be?

Although I may sound cynical, it is refreshing to see his enthusiasm. I've been here long enough to know that he will have his work cut out for him. Heck, he's thinking, these folks are almost in Heaven, just a little shove from him and they'll be there.

We are approaching an old fellow on a porch. He's planted quite firmly in his rocker, puffing away on his pipe. He removes the pipe and shouts, "Get the hell off my property, you lowlife scum!"

As Cliff assures him we've only come for a friendly visit, he reaches down and pulls out a shotgun. Of course he doesn't know it's just a thought form, but unfortunately it still manages to put the willies into young Cliff, who raises his arm and says, "Now there'll be no need for that, sir."

As our host continues to rant we turn to leave, and I tune into his past life. An estranged homosexual son, a wife who got religion real bad and left him, a farm repossessed. He's angry at God, he's angry at life, he's mad at himself.

I clap Cliff on the shoulder. "Shit happens, dude, even in the after-life."

He shakes his head and says, "Another time, my friend, another time."

We head back into town. Cliff spies a couple of ladies who seem to be sipping tea in their garden, nudges me, and walks over. They nod ever so slightly. They're dressed as if they'd gone to church one Sunday in May 1948 and just plum forgot to change.

Cliff bids them good day and I smile in support.

The lady on the left, seeing Cliff's Bible, says, "You're not Mormons, are you? Can't abide Mormons."

Cliff graciously declines.

"Well then, what are you? Catholics? They're even worse, screwing like rabbits and begging that Virgin Mary for favors."

Cliff declares us Christians bringing the message of peace and love.

"Peace and love, my ass, you're just looking for money like the rest of them. Now be off with you before I call the police." She glares at us unblinking. I sense she's protecting her companion, who sits noncha-lantly sipping. There's a philandering minister and a botched abortion in there somewhere, I can feel it.

Cliff hasn't relaxed enough to tune into other people's thoughts yet, not to mention that sympathetic telepathy is completely outside his belief system, so when I mention this a few steps later, he pooh-poohs in a tone that somehow suggests a suspicion of moral degeneracy. I tell him it's only black magic if you use it to manipulate people against their wishes. He smiles knowingly.

We enter, at his insistence, a dilapidated church that bears the psy-chic imprints of many a fundamentalist preacher. I feel hectored at every step. No one seems to be around. Cliff takes a pew. I watch him bend and pray. I do not feel the urge myself, but I respect his need for silence.

As he prays for strength and guidance, I watch the ray of light that descends to him from above. A streaky blend of white and violet, it enters at his crown chakra and spreads a slight glow throughout. I sense it is time to leave and move upward and inward.

My vibrations increase and I appear in a glowing meadow on the edge of a small wood. Foothills rising beyond are sculpted with terraced gardens that enrapture the unaccustomed eye: It's as if Virginia suddenly gave way to Tuscany. Some devoted and creative souls hereabouts.

A few steps through long caressing grasses, and I am beside a glistening murmuring brook. Just down the way some children are playing and splashing about. Confessions of laughter fill the air.

I float down towards the group, gliding about them as a seagull might on Earth, swooping and diving and generally dishing out the fun I feel in my heart. Since I've come over, I can't say anything gives me more pleasure than this. To feel childlike and carefree, moving with the will of the moment, mischievous as a breeze, this is my fragment's fulfillment.

The Summerland

This is, as some of you may have guessed, the "Summerland" made famous on Earth by the Spiritualists of the late-nineteenth and early-twentieth centuries, when it was basically all the rage. Séances and table rappings on every other street corner. Everyone's uncle coming through with tales of cigars and churches carved in gold.

And it was all righteously mocked by my day, when rationalism and science had delivered us from the twin horrors of starvation and plague safely into the arms of greedy consumption and nuclear annihilation.

Yes, this is the land of endless June, where happy families of every description relax into the longest and loveliest vacation imaginable. Many millions of souls reside here. Every nationality and religion is represented in a prodigious array of landscapes, archetypes from which devolve national dreams: the dreamy foothills of the Himalayas, the rocky sculptures of Arizona, the endless grasslands of Africa, the dramatic fiords of Scandinavia.

Soul types range from those with just a modicum of kindness and compassion, to those who on Earth would strictly regulate their behavior with moral codes and civilized conduct, to those whose hearts were just bursting with love and could barely contain themselves from embracing any stranger in the street.

Hereabouts, of course, most are former U.S. and Canadian citizens, neighbors on that longest undefended border. But as both countries encourage immigration, the astral planes above them embrace a wide assortment of racial types. Aside from religion, which, of course, binds many, their common heritage is what has become known as "pop culture." A fascinating amalgam of sports, television, movies, and music (which barely existed in my day), this endless well of knowledge, which some call trivia, joins many in a kind of postmortem obsession.

I can still recall my amusement when a teen suicide told me the thing she missed the most was Madonna. Another guy, a car-crash victim, wanted to know how he could catch the World Series. "All right, all right," I remember him saying in exasperation, "I believe you, I'm dead, but just get me to the Yankees, will ya?"

After buzzing about their frolics, I settle on the bank and smile. Children here are like children anywhere, endlessly inventive with their games. One child is effortlessly skimming the surface of the water, something like the dragonflies I remember from my youth, coming ever so close without actually touching it. His arms spread like wings, his face filled with grin. A laughing girl follows his example and would immediately succeed but for her loose skirts trailing in the water.

A new twist quickly develops: One boy waits for the skimmers to pass and neatly jumps over them as they do so, again coming close without touching. A competitive logic soon develops, and soon they're divided into two teams, skimmers and jumpers. For a time concentration quells laughter, but it does not last long. As if by remote control a mass collapse is engineered, followed by shrieks and splashing.

It's at times like this when I think of the astral plane as one of full-tilt fun. That was one of Veronica's sayings, when she was feeling gay and had lots of my money to spend. I resented it then, in my oh-so-sensible way, but sure see a good use for it now, as I observe the endless play of divine energies, chasing each other around and around this multi-layered universe of ours and learning, as they go, the rules of the game.

These children, I soon find out, belong to a village nearby. One of them offers to show me around. When I thank him for his kindness, he says it's okay, he has a music lesson soon anyway. He'd reached grade five piano by the time he bought it on the highway with three of the friends I'd seen at the river, and since it was the thing he loved most about his life, he's decided to keep it up. Stealing cars, gees, he'll never do that again.

Still, it could be worse. His grandparents are great to live with. They've been here a long time and are really in the swing of things, complete social butterflies, totally vibed from, well, it'd be morning to night if we were still on Earth, wouldn't it?

His parents are a bit more of a problem. Mum still hasn't climbed out of her depression and drinks way more than she should, and Dad just works all the time. He's tried over and over to talk with them when they're dreaming, and although they say they understand that they will meet him when they pass over, he sees them still stuck in the same old ruts and getting worse.

His guide tells him that his mother will soon be completely stuck on the physical plane if she keeps boozing the way she does. He's seen for himself the four or five drunks that have taken to hanging around her for the buzz and it scares the shit out of him.

We turn into a hamlet straight out of Vermont. There's even a bookstore in a converted barn. Like many settlements on this plane, it's an archetypal delight: a sleepy village patted into perfection by many loving hands and minds, the sort of spot half of America would give its right hand to live in and the other half considers a kind of Peyton Place Hell for the pretentious nouveau riche.

My new young friend says, "It's been nice talking to you, but I must go in here for my lesson," and walks up a garden path with a friendly wave. I see for the hundredth or so time why the mid-astral is so many people's idea of the perfectly civilized and polite society.

Sure families are split up in odd cross-generational patterns, but because of the much speeded-up sense of time, the thirty or so years Earth time spent glumly by those "left behind" seems like about five here, five years of what comes across as the most relaxing and yet stimulating vacation possible, five years of a whale of a time with the rest of the family fogged in at the airport. Or, as one recent resident said to me when asked how he was doing, "Man, it's like Barbados with the best libraries and museums ever!"

There's a village green, complete with pond, swans, overarching trees, and band shell. Two gentlemen are chuckling while they play chess. The ornately carved pieces are living testaments to an original artistic sensibility. They are, I am told, copies from a set designed by some famous European artist who came to the States during World War II.

Alex and Hershel are golfing partners from way back. Heck, they've been dead almost as long as me. They're 71 and 73 respectively. Alex from a heart attack after his Vietnam vet son committed suicide and Hershel from good old-fashioned cancer. Only Hershel's wife is here, and only just: She hung in till she was 89. Hershel thought she was nuts, all those years in that nursing home when she could've been here having fun. He tried to convince her God knows how many times while she was asleep. But she did love her grandchildren and her great-grandchildren. Hershel says it's the matriarch complex—convinced the ship of state can't run without you. Now she wants to enlarge the house to make more space for family when they come. Hershel tells her they can have their own houses, hell this place is bigger than Texas and New Mexico run together, but she's consulting with a renovator and interior designer now. She really is in Heaven, he laughs, but she still won't admit she shoulda come here sooner.

Alex's story turns on the reincarnation of his suicide son. He says he wouldn't have believed it if he hadn't seen it for himself. He has always been a Christian, if not always a churchgoing one. Had some problems with the pastor that really ticked him off. Anyway, he was a "one life and eternity" man until his son Wayne said he was going back to complete some unfinished business. Alex had been a budding artist when the draft disappeared him. And having helped to stem the tide of godless communism in Korea, he opposed his wife's plan to move to Canada and set up shop there. After all, she said, he was a bus driver and she a hairdresser, they could do that anywhere.

Of course, their age difference didn't help. Twenty-five when he returned from Korea, they met at a church social and fell hopelessly in love. She was only 17. Her parents not approving, they eloped and married when she turned 18 a few weeks later.

'Course she blamed him for Wayne's death and he stewed in his guilt. Their daughter had changed her name and run off to join a commune in California. His heart attack came suddenly and swiftly. In seconds he was facing an angel that claimed to be his guardian.

Well, to cut a long story short, he and Wayne, thanks to several helping hands, managed to find each other and then live together. But that same guardian angel had poisoned his boy's mind with thoughts of going back. In no time at all he was determined to be the baby his middle-aged mother was determined to have with her second husband. And by God they pulled it off with Shirley at 42.

Alex tells me he has certainly come around in his thinking and is now taking a course in world religions, that's along with his choir practice and anthropology course, of course. There's so much time for everything here, that's what he likes the most. On Earth there never seemed to be enough time for anything, you were so busy turning a buck and bringing up your kids. He's even figured out how to go to one of the lower astrals and visit his bad-tempered drunk of a father, who will still hear nothing of clean living and religion, he laughs.

And what am I doing here, he asks. I explain my project with Gordon. They are intrigued. Hershel had no idea giant rescue efforts were coordinated at natural disasters. He just hadn't given it a thought.

But now that he knows, hey, he'd like to help out. Just tell him where and when. Alex seems more interested in the channeling. I tell them I have to be off, but I shall return and spend some quality time.

Alex says the choir is working up Fauré's *Requiem,* if I can believe it. They're just a village choir, but they've managed to snag a few dead professionals who just fell in love with the neighborhood. In fact there are even a couple of gay guys if I'm interested. Now I'm not to take offense, it's just that it's the first time he's had a chance to get to know any. I tell him not to worry, there's no offense taken. In fact if he shows me where they live, I'll drop by and say hello. I'll have to admit I'm impressed they're doing the Fauré. It's a beautiful piece which requires much sensitivity and restraint.

I accept his gracious offer and make my farewells, this time walking to the edge of the village and finding the home of the gay couple empty before lifting off and floating to the nearest town.

It's about time I visited my girlfriend. You're right, some things never change, the wrath of a woman kept waiting being one. Okay, I exaggerate. She's not that bad. But she's really quite a stay-at-home girl—a weaver, a maker of tapestries, a reader of books. Medieval illustrated manuscripts are her current fascination; she'll pore over them for days in utter delight.

The libraries here can make fabulously accurate facsimiles of anything ever published on Earth, and quite a few things that never made it out of places like the Vatican library. Ancient Sanskrit texts to unpublished drafts of Bob Dylan songs, it's all here.

Most people can't believe it when they first visit. For lifetime library users, it's a dream come true. All of human history lies waiting for your lackadaisical perusal. I still get a charge from lolling around the stacks listening to first-timer's exaltations as they discover some "lost" work of Paracelsus or Sappho.

Think of all the people who have ever said to you, "Gee, I'd love to do such and such, if only I had the time." Well, they're all here studying something or other. It's a wonderful sight to see.

Anyway, my girlfriend is also a wonderful sight to see and I suppose that's why we're going there now. The beautiful hills and valleys of astral Vermont gradually give way to a rolling landscape of mixed woodland and meadow dotted with what can only be described as a beautiful variety of dwellings. Humble log cabins, ornate majestic mansions, shining steel and glass pyramids, geodesic domes covered in grass, all these are here, and more. More than enough for several spectacular issues of *Architectural Digest*.

The city shines ahead, as all cities do on this level. When you first arrive, fresh from the land of old age and winter gloom, you think it's the buildings that are shining. Then you refine that to, no, they're emitting light, they're glowing. Then you see the people are, too. And the trees. And the flowers. And the rivers.

Then you realize that it comes with the territory. When you exist on this level, you shine. And then, after a while, you get used to it and don't notice any more. Right now I'm making myself notice for your benefit. I hope you're appreciating it.

I think you've realized by now that there are very few vehicles here. People stroll, float, or think themselves to places. I'm floating so that you can enjoy some of the view. Vehicles are still maintained by those who love the thought of them. Vintage car lovers have their rallies here just as they did on Earth. Horse and buggy fanciers do the same. Skiers ski in the mountains; water skiers do the same on lakes.

But nobody *needs* these methods of transport. They're much-loved habits extended here for fun. As one set of dead people grows out of their Earth-bound ways and look to more refined applications of their ever-expanding talents, another set appears to take up the slack. As on Earth, the graduating class always has its replacements.

As this town has a pleasant avenue leading up to a rather impressive Gothic-style archway, I shall continue the narrative at a walking pace. The grass beneath my feet is as velvety soft as anywhere on this plane. On first arrival its caress on the bare soles can induce ecstasies in the unsuspecting.

Of course for an astral sophisticate like me it's all rather old hat. To bliss out I now need the vibrations of the upper mental/lower causal plane. Don't be confused, we'll get to that a little later, I promise. But the last point has reminded me of something I've been meaning to get to for a while now, this notion of getting accustomed to the various levels of postmortem bliss and feeling the urge to move on. If it seems redolent of the psychology of addiction, then you're joining my thought.

After several years (Earth time) of perusing the lower planes for possible retrievals (i.e., those ready to relinquish their obsessive fears and limiting belief systems), it occurred to me that, in the worlds of form, maybe addictions are all we have.

For instance, here in the mid-astral, this summerland of sumptuous beauty and heartfelt ease, certain addictions are quite okay. If, say, you can't get through the day without either listening to or performing music; reading or writing a book; creating or reacting to art; practicing science or philosophy; worshiping God or one of her many cohorts; building, renovating, or decorating a house; putting your heart into your (or someone else's) garden; or just generally communing with nature, then this surely is the place for you, for these and other such addictive habits are honored here.

Addictions such as war, depression, heroin, alcohol, tobacco, money, power, and sex are frowned upon and will only (I can guarantee) keep you relegated to those dense areas close to, or even below, the physical plane. And if you insist on continuing to practice these "wrong" addictions, I can assure you, as I've so often heard on my trips back to Earth, you will be "shit out of luck" as far as bettering yourself goes.

Now, of course, on this level, the mid-astral, where by far the largest number of souls dwell, it is not commonly realized that the habits that they most admire and promote are the very ones that they will have to relinquish if they wish to make further progress. The upper reaches of Heaven, you see, are quite formless, and the houses, gardens, personalities, and cultures that we so carefully cultivate on our way up, as it were, must be ruthlessly cast aside in order to participate in the new ballgame of pure mind. Mind without form, mind eternal and unending.

Naturally I do my best to illuminate these thorny issues, but as the mid-astral is filled to the brim with competing belief systems and agendas, and many of these believers see the glorious worlds of form to be the ultimate achievement, my words often fall on stony ground and I am often seen as some renegade huckster spoiling the fun.

[But the final revelation, I must emphasize, after all the pleasant surprises of eternal life and endless fun have settled in—and it's the one most souls have trouble with—is that ultimately we have no bodies at all.]

[Our "higher selves," that eternal identity that has been pulling us slowly up through the planes, is essentially a formless, genderless accumulation of light energy, which can, at the slightest flicker of will, be anything and go anywhere. Cultures and personalities are mere files on its hard drive.]

[But unfortunately, when a soul has swallowed the religious propaganda of its culture and epoch to the point where it completely blocks out the knowledge of its eternal and absolute freedom unencumbered by saviors, creeds, and deities, it condemns itself to dwell in the postmortem paradises of the various prophets—still in a body and still worshiping a separate God—when in fact, in its truest self, that spirit exists beyond definition in complete and utter union with the divine.]

Oneness or Limitlessness

Henry and Guinevere

Henry and Guinevere: sounds like an unlikely match for a couple, I know, but a couple we are and have been for quite some time, as the saying goes.

It is said that opposites attract, and that is certainly the case with us. Me, the multidimensional rover, ranging through the planes like some divinely inspired clown, and she the calm industrious artisan, content to remain within her community, creating the tapestries that grace the homes of her friends and fans.

We first met in Renaissance Venice as what I believe are now called sex-trade workers. In those days it was, among other things, the only way a woman could get a half-decent education and her hands anywhere near the reins of power. As courtesans catering to a wealthy clientele, we often found ourselves at the same parties and dinners, and it was not long before a mutual attraction exposed itself.

We lived as secret lovers for many years, eventually retiring to share a home in our old age. Not wishing to be separated by the death of one, we sought and found a poison we could share. Needless to say, we were not buried in sacred ground. We didn't care. We'd both serviced enough prelates in our day to see the ecclesiastical conspiracy for what it was: fear clinging to power. Besides, we were together in spirit and happy as kids at a picnic, what did we care for burials and society's approval?

Our blissful astral interlude was ended, as they often are, by karmic obligations knocking at the door. Dutiful souls, we delved into our respective businesses, for we each have many lines of development to follow, and were not brought together again until turn-of-the-century Boston, when, as you've heard, as brother and sister we scampered the carpets of a luxurious nursery, with my sister, Ann, as governess. Unfortunately, a careless cook burned the place to the ground, and our poor little bodies perished in the flames.

That was enough for Martha, as she was called then, and she would not take another life, as I did, in the 1920s. What a joy it was to rediscover her, when Ann, disguised as Phoebe, brought her around for a visit a week or so after I passed, and it was love at twentieth sight, as some of us say up here. This little story alone will show you how much I've changed in my "time" here.

I think on these things and more as I saunter along a tree-lined hallway that curves and meanders in a way no Earthly one would dare. Large glass panels in the wall intermittently reveal a miniature rain forest masquerading as the grounds for this condominium complex, as I believe you now call them on Earth. There's even a controlled rain shower every once in a while to maintain that much-needed clammy and drippy effect so beloved by rain forest fans.

Curlicues of sherry-colored light announce some music from one of the rehearsal areas. As the complex is mainly populated by artists of all kinds, there are several rehearsal spaces where people can polish up their skills as various passers-by slow to bend an eye or ear.

Yes, it's the same original-instrument string quartet I saw on my last visit. They're playing the beautiful "Contrapuntus 5" from J. S.

Bach's *Art of the Fugue* in rich, rounded tones that seem to take the edge off my ardor. I sit on a bench and burrow into the beauty. When they finish, I look up and nod my approval.

Mark, one of the violinists, says, "Better than last time, eh Henry?"

I laugh and shrug. He tells me if I'm here to visit Guinevere I'm out of luck. He saw her a while back and she was off to visit Rachel on the other side of town. And as she and Rachel are, shall I say, the best of friends, I know she'll not be back anytime soon.

Just what I deserve, I guess. I've been so preoccupied with giving you the guided tour I neglected to send a message. Guinevere's very set that way. She likes the old social etiquettes, one of which is the telepathic calling card before your arrival.

Oh well, we'll go to her rooms and I'll reenact an intimate encounter. Now, that I have permission for. It's been okayed. Not with enthusiasm but with a certain dedication to the cause.

We felt it was important that you understand how loving souls achieve union on this plane. Well, I felt it; Guinevere was a little slower to come around. The general idea she was certainly in favor of; it was the illustrative details she was loathe to divulge. I assured her we would not be making a sex video, or even a brochure advertising one.

She did not want Rachel mentioned at all, for despite being a spiritual entity filled with love for all in her ken, she retains some very nineteenth-century ideas about sexuality. And never having been an adult in the twentieth, the age of sexual emancipation, that's not surprising really, is it?

I assured her that frank sex talk is quite acceptable now on Earth, and homosexual relations all the rage. Certainly in North America and Europe lesbians are very chic. But as she does not take such an active interest in Earthly affairs as I, she found this all very hard to believe. Now having Rachel as her "sister lover," as she puts it, you might think this all a touch precious, but you must understand Guinevere's notions of sexuality come from an earlier epoch, where courtly charm and chivalrous discretion gilded a multitude of sins.

Now as to our amours: kisses and caresses and whispered declarations of devotion, all these are as eternal as the peals of giggles that used to accompany nocturnal fumblings on Earth, and just as enjoyed. Penetrative intercourse, however, is a thing of the past, at least on this level. On the lower levels, due to blind lust and lack of imagination mostly, it still holds a certain sway. But here, a blending of heart chakra energies can be achieved, and when it is, the lovers are blessed with a blissful union in which every cell in their bodies seems animated with an orgasmic flush that surges and resurges until smoothed by a pleasing exhaustion.

Now, my young suicide lovers we encountered a while back, they're probably bonking furiously every chance they get, even though I've warned them that conception is impossible here, but when I (or someone else for that matter) show them the heart chakra blending technique, there'll be no turning back, I can assure you.

[There is also a blending of the crown chakra available for those brave enough to try. I say brave, as the experience can be so blissfully overwhelming as to obliterate all notion of personality for quite some time, and that's an experience not many can cope with. They still want to be who they are, and as I previously explained, that habit can really hold you back here.]

I hope such bald-faced discussion of astral plane sexuality has not offended anyone, but I am determined to break the hold religionists have had on channeled communications for the last century or so. The poor souls meant well, but they managed to convey totally erroneous notions of asexual angels gliding about praising the lord and doing good works, when in fact, most souls are very sensual here, as joy is constantly in the air and there are no strictures or punishments for acting out your desires.

No disease, no pregnancy, no shame.

The Mental Plane

Entire ch.

In a nutshell this is the area where souls think things over. Not that they didn't think during either their Earthly or astral sojourns—they did, depending, of course, on ability and desire. But here they have no heavy bodies or bubbling emotions to distract them. Here there is only thought: the power of it, the beauty of it, the very life of it.

[On the astral there is plenty of "time" to study and reflect, whether it be on the evolution of the family as an interactive learning unit or the relationship of architecture and music, but there is still a sense of the student and that which is studied.

Here there is little or no such distinction. Souls absorb thought as flowers absorb sunlight. To think a thought is to enter into it wholly and completely, to understand its history and revere its passage through many minds towards completion.

For an example, take the thought "democracy." Savor it like a scholar of political science and history with endless grant monies to fund his speculation. Examine it as a jeweler would a rare diamond. Check every reference in every encyclopedia. See how it was used on other planets. Check in with Aristotle and Plato. Ask Freud if it was all some sort of sexual neurosis. Play around with the evolution of the city state; see one as a function of the other.

Do all this while meditating on what seems like one very pleasant afternoon in the garden of your new home on the mental plane, for this is where you will have graduated to upon relinquishing your astral body. This used to be called the "second death," but that all seems a bit melodramatic now.⌋

After a refreshing splash in the river, which will no doubt be running not far away, you return to consider the idea of "compassion." Its uses and abuses. Its role in family and society. Its moral value in religions. The extent to which it can be used as a barometer of soul growth. Its merit, say, as a bridge between islands. Its perversion into sickly sentimentality. Its great value in promoting self-esteem amongst its practitioners.

Just as on Earth, there are discussion groups to join, lectures to listen to, and studies to undertake. But here it can all be done without "stepping outside." Merely thinking deeply on any subject will deliver the thinker into an animated vortex of ever-multiplying ideas, as if she were interacting with many others instead of stretching sleepily on her couch.

Many souls, lacking the necessary development, pass through this plane half asleep, or even completely asleep. The intensity of the vibrations is basically too much and they cope by shutting down. Imagine an eight-year-old lost in a university, wandering into classrooms and labs without a clue, and you've got the picture. Now imagine a 14-year-old in the same position. Think of the bits and pieces she might manage to amass before feeling lost and sleepy.

Of course each soul absorbs what it can. Capacities vary and generally increase with the number of lives intelligently lived. Now someone out there will want me to define "intelligently lived." I can just hear the ripples rolling around. I mean lives expended in the conscious expansion of capabilities, lives where talents are stretched and generously shared.

The surrounding landscapes are as varied and beautiful as those in the astral just visited, only more so. To shift from the upper astral to the lower mental is to be dazzled as much as the move from the physical to the astral. What I can say is, it just keeps getting better. And the bliss refines itself as you approach.

[And I might add, no one takes the transition until they are ready. There is no wrenching of hearts. And those who go on can always come back for visits. Those who already know about higher selves and development through reincarnation generally understand just which part of the eternal cycle they are on, while those who believe in the "one life and then eternity" scenario think they're moving to a higher plane, closer to the saints and deities they revere. And by this point in the journey there is little bickering, although there are definitely groups gathered together studying the finer points of comparative religion.]

While everyone has their own creed-defined Heaven in the upper astral—and I mean everyone, not just the big names in the mental plane—worship has a much more ecumenical tone. The most open-minded Christians and Moslems will pray together, and Hindus and Buddhists will share the same temples, to name but two examples. And yes, theosophists and spiritualists can still be found debating the doctrines of karma and reincarnation as vigorously as on Earth, although I must point out that the debate, shorn of its lower and more competitive emotions, is quite sparkling in its refinement.

Beyond this level, and beyond what is technically another death—the third if you're counting—but what is really nothing more than a slow easy fading into what can best be described as a warm affectionate light, lie the formless planes, called by some Buddhic, by others celestial, and by yet others nirvanic.

But what's in a name, I can hear you all saying, warming to the task of no-task about as well as I did when I first discovered the promise of easy disintegration was all that was left at the end of the rainbow. The big leap into nothingness some call it, usually as they try to work up the nerve.

Well you can't blame them really. After all those exciting adventures in the world of buildings, food, and bodies, or "chasing, catching, and losing," as I like to call it, nothingness seems a bit of a letdown, even if it is a void brimming with potential and ecstasy beyond compare.

People really do get used to the way they look and are often loathe to give it up for the promise of what—the thrill of endless anonymity in a sea of anonymity? Doesn't sound so fantastic, does it? *Correct*

[Ah, but when you get there the bliss just blows you away. Reuniting with your higher self, that depository of all your other personalities, can be like checking into the grandest of grand hotels, where everyone you meet is your oldest and closest friend and where the backslapping party stops only for your momentary reentry.] *The Higher Self or Self*

[At least, that's what someone told me as they headed back down through the planes for another stab at perfecting themselves in the school of hard knocks. As for myself, I've yet to take that particular plunge.]

And if I had, I wouldn't be able to talk to you now as Henry, as he would've long been engulfed by a much greater reality encompassing all his lives on Earth and would be barely recognizable as a human soul at all. And his higher self, like all higher selves, which never actually incarnates at all but merely sends down exploratory missions to report back to base, would have seemed quite remote and forbidding, a faceless bureaucrat with little interest in your earnest enquiries, a monumental accumulation of experiential detail devoid of the human warmth and frailty we all so like to see in each other.

[For instead of all that human stuff, it glows like a white onion lit from the inside by a huge floodlight, its surface sparkling with bands of brilliant colors revealing a constant shifting of textures and hues, which always seem to me like the visual equivalent of giggling.

Now make no mistake, there is no substance to these beings, unless you consider beams of light substantial. They are energy in its purest state, "isness unbounded," as a friend of mine once said.]

And speaking of friends, I've organized a little meeting for you all, back down on the mid-astral where I hang all my hats, and we'd better hightail it before the guests start grumbling.

All Back to My Place

Of course it takes but a second for me to shift here, so I hope you're comfortable with the fact that we're walking through the garden towards the front door. Inside we're going to meet an assortment of my friends who are all, in one way or another, spirit guides to various souls on Earth. I thought you might be interested in the wide variety of their experiences.

It was Gordon who first suggested it, way back when, but his astral recall is so weak I doubt that he'll remember it, leaving me to take the credit as his all-wise, all-loving guardian.

Well here they are, all in the den, doing what they do best, acting like fools. What can I say, it's the pressure of the job; either you're roundly ignored for years, and often decades, or you're worshiped beyond all reason and made into some minor deity. Either way, acting like fools is often a great release.

So that's why Sunil and Randy are hanging from those wooden

beams, and Charity, Virginia, Lloyd, Hester, Bruno, and Julia are on
their hands in a three-two-one pyramid. I hope you can visualize the
scattershot antics as they fall and unroll, full of merry laughter.

Sunil's first off the mark, says he's in a bit of a hurry to get back, but
he wants to talk shop about computer software, one of his specialties. I
warn him off the technical details and he launches into a description of
the three high-tech whiz-kids he's working with, developing an inex-
pensive hand-held computer/videophone/entertainment center that
should be on the market about 2004.

There's Sheila, the dressed-for-success redhead, married with one
child, a genius control freak with a twisted heap of denied emotions on
the other side of the wall. Then Edward, the wayward son of an appeals
court judge, smart as a whip and manipulative as hell. Got about five
women in knots trying to tie him down, and the usual cache of unresolved conflicts with his mother. And last but not least, Emil, a bisexual
wunderkind who can seduce anyone except his own sense of inadequacy.

All three, says Sunil, mistake self-interest for kindness and advance
their careers convinced they're great humanitarians. The constant tur-
moil of near genius is, of course, their great excuse. Aside from the software R&D, Sunil's specialty is the subtleties of moral choice facing
modern man.

Do they face more choice than medieval man or ancient man? He
thinks so. The freedom of the individual in modern secular society is
unparalleled in history. And that means the freedom to make choices
rather than following rules or customs.

Every time Sheila uses her charm and glamour (bewitching eyes
and fabulous legs), Sunil is at her shoulder reminding her she promised not to do this and how disappointed she was in herself last time
around when she finally admitted how sexually manipulative she had
been. She knows it's a lack of self worth that propels this, but her initial motivation for change has been muddied by her continued success
in the art.

Now Edward, he's a classic user. So smart, he sees through everyone's game in minutes and spends the rest of the relationship turning them on a spit of their own illusions and actively enjoying the roasting. Sunil keeps trying to nudge him up a notch where he can use his sharp insights to help people stretch beyond their foolish limitations, and it's so frustrating because Edward is so close to turning over that new leaf that Sunil can almost smell it.

Emil, of course, is libido incarnate, a serpent of desire in a garden of breeding. His specialty is to take married people of both sexes and, by igniting their passions, show them how bored they are. As a former lady of pleasure myself, I understand all too well how this gift can deteriorate from a high pinnacle of divine subversiveness into an egotistical display of lascivious dexterity.

Sunil says thanks, you've stolen my best line. Everyone chuckles: My past lives are as much an open book as theirs, and at least two people present were my clients in that far epoch. And Guinevere, as you know, was a big part of that life too, but she prefers not to talk about it, saying that apart from her commitment to me, it's pretty much a closed book for her.

Now Charity, she's a classic Cupid-style guide, nudging old soul mates out of their orbits just enough to collide with their unfinished bits and pieces of karma. She freely admits it's the type of task that puts her earlier obsession with love and romance to good use. "I'm a love junkie, what can I say?" is her favorite justification, and another indication of this influx of pop-culture terminology in the last thirty or so years Earth time. When I was alive, so to speak, junkies were one thing and one thing only: heroin addicts.

As she describes her cast of characters, her love for them and the machinations she engineers to get them to face their old hurts and energy blockages is obvious. That she relishes the endless challenges is plain.

Now Dorothy, remember, she's the one who's been trying for years to pluck up her nerve to leave her successful but stultifying husband

and travel. The usual guilt and timidities have kept her housebound and childless for years, but a small inheritance from an aunt she could barely remember revived the old itch, and with a silent word or two from Charity, she was off.

To San Francisco—which from Cleveland seemed like the most exciting destination without going international—where she was nudged to stay in a certain hotel just down the block from a favorite watering spot of an old nemesis, now called Dennis.

Now what is assumed by us in this discussion, and what should be made explicit to you readers, is that Dorothy's lifetime spirit guardian, the one she chose before birth, had contacted Charity some months before and told her of Dorothy's oft-expressed wish to be more bold in love this time around.

Such a course of action is not uncommon. Guides have their specialties: Some work with compassion, some with power issues, others with envy and jealousy, some with fear and anger, some with healing, some with technical research. Some, of course, are just general all-purpose guides, lifetime companions who turn to specialists at certain significant junctures.

Charity informs us (much to our amusement, as Dorothy has for years proved immune to the promptings of her lifetime guide) that for some reason Charity cannot fathom, Dorothy has been easily led to meet up with Dennis, who, in his usual fashion, had her in bed within the hour, for what she described as "a sweatfest beyond her wildest dreams."

Now what Charity would like to see is Dorothy emerging from her cocoon to take flight as a proudly orgasmic woman of the twentieth century, who will cruise through affairs gaining, not losing, momentum. Even the gynecological impasse was engineered with this in mind. But will she survive Dennis's customary petty betrayals and push through to the wiser character beyond? This is what Charity would have us root for.

Sunil asks about Dorothy's brother Lawrence: How is he coping?

We all know his partner Gavin took on AIDS this time around and that the last few weeks had been almost too much for him. Charity reports that Lawrence is still very much bound in grief over his loss, which from her point of view is ironic, as Gavin is as close to him as ever, hanging around the house as he does, hoovering up all Lawrence's emotions like some hungry orphan.

Which, in a way, he is, she continues to muse, as he steadfastly ignores all his spiritual relations in favor of his last Earthly one. A not uncommon problem amongst obsessives, unfortunately. And, as we've all heard from Charity before, this is not the first time these two souls have been thusly enmeshed. As widowed mother and only son and twin brothers orphaned by fire, they have earlier sought the world only in each other. Between lives, of course, they came to see their mutual devotion as a limiting folly, but as incarnate egos they easily slip into the same old patterns.

Charity has, in fact, just come from another fruitless spell of Gavin watching. She chuckles as she says this, explaining that she can never get Gavin to so much as glance at her, his focus is so confined. The very definition of Earth-bound, I suggest, and Sunil accuses me once again of taking all the best lines. I apologize and offer to swap scripts with him.

Now Karen, Charity's other major interest, is really making strides. A typical conventional soul who usually abides by her society's and family's expectations, she has, for once, fulfilled her fantasy instead of denying it. Charity's not sure whether her psychic whispers of encouragement did the trick or not, but she assures us she certainly put enough effort into it over the months.

Virginia asks if this means bisexuality. Charity answers it certainly does. Karen, after her usual habit of mulling it over for about a decade, has initiated a fling with her neighbor Helen. Helen, a somewhat worn veteran of such amours, has been totally charmed by Karen's blushing enthusiasm and is happy to assume the passenger seat for a change.

This is one case where deceit can have its champions, Charity argues. Karen's confidence in herself has blossomed dramatically, for the first time in several lives. Besides, husband Ben would really rather not know. Heavens, chirps in Julia, the next thing you know she'll be taking night courses.

Our chuckles may seem cruel, but believe me, our collective patience is much tried. Incarnate humans can be incredibly reluctant to change their ancient ways, despite their prebirth pleadings for just such assistance.

Now Virginia, having been both a politician and a politician's wife, understands the temptations of that very slippery territory and, not surprisingly, in this astral interim, has volunteered herself for guardian duties amongst the rich and powerful. Ever dangling on the precipices of power, these souls risk much in what has been termed their "evocation of ambition."

First off she has Lloyd, an aging senator with a preference for sloppy accounting and a weekend penchant for cross-dressing. The latter, Virginia feels, is actually quite beneficial on a soul level, as it allows him the expression, albeit limited, of a gentler side of his nature, and without which, she is sure, he would slide right off some deep end she doesn't want to deal with. So yes, she gives him every encouragement.

But not so with the frauds, those filchings from the public purse practiced with such frequency and ease that Virginia now sees them as a rock solid character trait and not the passing fancy she first imagined.

By witnessing the parade of his motivations and justifications, she thinks it all boils down to two factors. First, his deep sense of lack of appreciation of his commitment and lifetime efforts; and second, a deep-seated desire towards dishonesty for its own sake, which springs, she believes, from a religious upbringing whose overemphasis on the good made being wicked seem wildly attractive. But yes, she admits, Lloyd has chosen such religious persuasion time and time again, revealing what can only be, to her, an inadequate sense of his own moral stature.

Virginia says she would love to see him leap right over all conventional notions of good and bad but realizes the virtual impossibility of that this time around. But there is still no reason for him to get stuck at the bad-boy stage. She wants him to relinquish all the secret thrills of a spanking and act dispassionately for the benefit of all. She thinks you readers understand the relativity of moral values but wants you to know that as a guide one comes to see the completely illusory nature of moral judgments. Ultimately you see there is no right or wrong, merely action with varying degrees of premeditation.

The only judgment is that issued by the individual's conscience, but as you now know, the spirit world is one created and sustained by thought, so judgments being thoughts, they can have a mighty effect on one's life and environment. Hopefully, Lloyd will have stopped judging himself by the time he gets here, which, if he doesn't start exercising pronto, will be sooner than he thinks.

Virginia's other charge is a head of state who will, for the sake of this project, remain nameless. A statesman by nature but ambitious dealmaker by trade, he suffers constantly from his inability to balance the two sides of his nature, and the resulting surges of energy are channeled into hasty sexual liaisons of a quite temporary nature.

Virginia, naturally, strives to effect a more natural balance where ideals can eventually be achieved through—rather than in spite of—the backroom deals that always comprise the underbelly of any international summit. The sexual liaisons, she feels, are not that significant, in that the correspondents are the type who thrill at the touch of power and are not otherwise adversely affected. Of course, her charge revels in his guilt, making quite a race of it with his spouse, who has many of her own illicit loves.

A far from uncommon state in politics, Virginia muses. She and her last spouse were similarly embroiled back in the thirties, and she remembers just how easily they slipped into competition. From dewy-eyed lovers to snarling rivals in about five years, she fondly recalls.

Randy, standing over her in a parody of solemnity, begs to differ, and if you could hear the way he says "my dear" you'd laugh as much as the rest of us. He wants to remind her of when he was the put-upon wife, knee deep in children, and she the philandering husband, but knowing what it will lead to I officially request him to keep to the agenda: souls you are currently guiding.

Sunil stands and begs our forgiveness. There's a conference coming up with at least two politically motivated seductions planned, and he wants to be close to the action. Not for the thrill of the conquest, Heavens, no. What do we take him for, a mere idle spectator? No, he has high moral standards he wishes to see upheld. Fat chance, Julia smirks, and we all laugh as he disappears.

Randy reports on his little criminals, as he calls them. Definitely a cast of unsavory characters by Earthly standards, but as I think I've said before, you meet all sorts in this line of work, and telling the bad guys from the good ones gets progressively more difficult as the lives roll by. As Randy likes to say, everyone's got a story to tell, and they all need some help telling it.

First off he gives us an update on Karl, the East German refugee smuggler and gun runner. In an attempt to learn dignity and humility through deprivation, Karl took a life in the tatters of post-war Germany, but the plan backfired and instead of becoming a pastor with a rock solid sense of mission he quickly blossomed into a petty criminal of above-average cunning, whose contacts in the East Berlin secret police soon led to smuggled bodies and arms shipments.

The age of computers and cell phones has given him a market of almost unlimited possibilities and citizenship on a planet just begging for plunder. Randy reminds us he lost contact with Karl many years ago but announces there's fresh hope on the horizon. Karl suddenly wants out and has decided in his world there's only one way: suicide. This has brought on bouts of depression, mostly booze soaked, but some deeply soul searching, and during one of these Randy managed a brief but successful appearance as the Angel of Death. Which, of course, he most definitely is not. But as I told you there is much playacting going on at this level, usually to conform to the soul's unconscious expectations.

Randy is happy to report that Karl had the shit properly scared out of him and immediately, and he means immediately, started giving money to charities, and specifically took a week or two off for a slave-freeing trip to Africa.

A hearty round of applause and Randy takes a bow. Virginia can't resist rubbing herself all over him in a parody of sexual submission. Moralists among you will be glad to know they live together here as a couple.

Of course these signs of weakness are a red flag in Karl's world. A poison dart or car bomb would seem imminent. But Randy hopes for some serious karma retooling before then.

Randy was first led to Karl through his work with Greg, a New York immigration lawyer, who has, over the years, uncovered many enterprising ways to establish citizenship for those with less-than-savory pasts. Everyone wants to come to the land of opportunity and Greg doesn't see why those on the fringes of respectability should be denied the chance. This line of work has led him into some fairly smoky backrooms, which Randy claims to find morally repugnant, even for someone with his kind of pasts. This, of course, gets a few laughs, as we all know his trail of political scandals. There's no possibility of hiding dirty laundry here.

Greg's motivation is what concerns Randy the most. Is he truly trying to help someone, or is he constantly ogling the size of the fee? Phony signatures and fraudulent documents aside, Randy claims to feel an increase in what he calls Greg's sensitivity to spiritual issues. He actually feels he is helping people to better themselves. Both Virginia and I have suggested, none too subtly, that he is flogging a dead horse and deluding himself in the bargain. Randy instinctively feels a measure of friendly rivalry in these comments and persists with his insistence that Greg is inching toward some semblance of moral respectability.

I accuse him of devising some ingenious new way of calculating the increments of ethical progress. He reminds me that his decades of political life have given him a unique perspective on the notion of corruption. He makes the analogy that as decay is present in all forms of growth, so too is corruption present in all forms of ethical endeavor.

Virginia interjects to suggest that Sunil should still be here to see that Henry doesn't always get the best lines. I invent a momentary hat (pork pie) and tip it in her direction. Everyone laughs.

Randy adds that as Greg is now being eagerly sought by some Russian mobsters, whose papers were not, shall we say, adequately convincing, we should pray for the state of his soul.

Julia works with children, if as she says you can call working with children work. Their playful spirits, as yet only slightly bruised from the brutishness of life, are a constant joy to be around.

All her charges live in the same neighborhood and go to the same school. An unusual circumstance to be sure, but fascinating if it can be arranged. In this case, a handful of Vietnam vets who died together in the jungle, ostensibly as the result of one shell. However, a deeper examination revealed a chain of similar sacrifices in other countries and other wars, the most recent, not surprisingly, being the American Civil War. Give some souls a nation, or a set of idealistic notions, to die for, and off they will go, time and time again, in the full binge of youth, to embrace death and glory.

None of them have made it past 25 in any male incarnation. So that's why they're all girls this time, Julia reminds us, to see if they can forgo the gusto of adventure for the domestic pleasures of children and garden. So far, Julia smirks, they're not doing too badly. They all like to wear dresses and play with dolls and think boys are stinky. Emily, Francis, Meagan, Diane, and Shelley: The little queens of junior kindergarten, Julia calls them. She can see them running the school by grade seven.

There's not a lot for Julia to do as yet, besides curbing their natural tendencies to envy, petty malice, and cliquish teasing. As before, Emily and Meagan are the leaders, Diane the beauty, Francis and Shelley the bridesmaids. Complete feminine makeovers of their previous male roles. But this time the adventure will be marriage, their cherished ideals beautiful homes, and their devotion to nation a devotion to family. And as grandmothers they will graduate to the gracious pose of wisdom, proffering the timeless advice to which youth usually remains resistant.

An interesting situation is developing, however. Emily is experiencing the bubbling up of memory fragments—the jungle at night, the palpable fear, the camaraderie, the thrill of choppers coming to the rescue. And she's telling her mother about a soldier named Dan and his four friends in the jungle.

Julia is not sure how to proceed: She is so concerned that they all experience a full life this time, and she doesn't want anything getting in the way. It certainly wasn't supposed to work out like this. Virginia suggests that she let things run their natural course. "Which is what?" asks Julia.

Which is either the memories will be explored or denied, but either way they will fade with time. Remember time, Virginia chuckles, that thing they do down there? Well, there's no denying that, I add, relieved that it's far from the best line.

We discuss the possible ramifications of Julia's concerns and conclude it's not worth worrying about. Julia just has to tend her garden like the rest of us, spreading fertilizer, pulling weeds, and watering when the time seems right.

A Chorus of Rescues

Lloyd, Hester, and Bruno want to tell you about some of the retrievals they've been involved in recently. They often work together as a team, sometimes using incarnate OBEs and sometimes not. Let's face it, Lloyd says, they're not always available when you need them.

But the situation is definitely getting better. With places like The Monroe Institute turning out graduates month after month, availability is becoming less and less of a problem.

Lloyd tells of a solo outing. He was just out cruising the suburbs one afternoon, watching gardeners and playing children, when he had an urge to check inside a house. Invaders of privacy we are not, I might add, but our intuitions about souls needing assistance are usually right on.

Sure enough, in the study stood a balding middle-aged man staring at his body slumped across a desk. The paperwork suggested an insurance agent or accountant. Lloyd could tell it was gonna be a toughie by the way he was staring at himself in disbelief.

An overweight 61 with about three too many bad habits and an almost textbook attitude of denial on all fronts: This is how Lloyd sums him up. I'm sure you've all known the type.

Lloyd's initial efforts at communication were completely ignored, and he wound up following the fellow around the house as the man tried to figure out why he couldn't grasp anything. Anger mounting, the man thought of his wife. And of course, the thought took him immediately to her presence, which was, much to his shock, in the arms of her lover in some utterly strange bedroom. Lloyd watched helplessly as the man's anger increased tenfold.

Blows to the boyfriend, of course, were useless. The man watched in amazement as his fist went right through the boyfriend's face and the pillow below. Cuckolded by that plain Jane! He was outraged. Lloyd again followed him about this new house as he tried to kick and punch things.

As a lifelong materialist, the man had virtually no road maps to the new territory he was now exploring. Nightmare was the best metaphor he could come up with. And when, oh when, was it all going to end, Lloyd could feel him thinking.

None too soon, as it turned out. He thought next of his own mistress, a real estate agent with a taste for bondage games. Lloyd could feel the pleasure rising in his charge. Suddenly they were in another house following a rather pretty fortyish woman as she pitched a sale to a couple of doctors.

Names became apparent: Hugh tried to gain Magda's attention, waving his arms in the air and claiming he'd never lied to her. Lloyd took this to refer to some earlier dispute. Then Hugh tried to importune the doctors: No luck there either. He flopped on a couch and began to whimper. Quite out of character, Lloyd was sure, but as I've mentioned before, we see all sorts of strange and gruesome sights in this line of work and are quite used to dramas of one sort or another. For us it's generally only slightly more involving than your average daytime soap opera.

A Chorus of Rescues

This detachment allowed Lloyd to come up with an idea. As Hugh whimpered himself into a state of numbed dejection, Lloyd joined his consciousness to him and whisked them both back to Hugh's house, where he left Hugh lying on his own bed. Back on this plane, Lloyd quickly found Hester reading in her garden and, explaining the situation, suggested a plan. Hester got a quick look at Magda's manner and gestures and the kind of games she liked to play with Hugh.

Fine-tuning her form, she appeared in front of Hugh in a slinky outfit and asked him if he wanted to come and play awhile. Lloyd says it was the husky voice that did it; a perfect imitation, he claims. Hester says it was nothing. We all laugh, knowing that impersonation is one of her specialties. Although a housewife and mother in her last life, she was a keen participant in local amateur theatre and finds what she calls her meager skills can be put to much greater use in this sphere of activity.

Needless to say, Hugh was successfully tempted into the afterlife, where after being led on a merry chase by Hester as Magda, he realized something was quite different and begged an explanation. Well, he'd had so much fun chasing Hester around, he almost didn't seem to care that he was dead, and when she dropped him off at the most suitable reception center, she made sure he got an eyeful of all the bikini-clad women basking about the pool before she bade him farewell.

Hester adds that for her that is still the most rewarding part of the job: when the doubting dead see just how much fun the afterlife is going to be and they get a grin a mile wide. Then, of course, she can go back to her garden and her book and exult in the knowledge of a job well done.

Bruno wants to talk about a couple of homeless men he and Lloyd have been working on for a while. They found them on a city sidewalk sleeping over a hot-air grate. Sadly the hot air had not been quite hot enough for them to escape the fate of exposure. They had been deceased for at least a day or so but remained so ignorant of their true condition that their many-layered outfits of ragged old clothes still seemed absolutely necessary, and as talking to each other fulfilled their meager social requirements, many of the customary indicators had passed unnoticed.

When one awakened, more from the habit of sleep than its actuality, Bruno made sure he was glowing with sufficient goodwill to create an angelic perception. The man noticed right away and alerted his companion to their new status. Bruno recalls his exact words: "Hey, Charlie, wake up, we must be dead, there's angels here."

Charlie proved to be as affable as his friend, who introduced himself as Vern, and asked, quite straight-faced, if they had anything decent to drink. Bruno chuckled and apologized, they'd forgotten to bring any along, but they could perhaps pick some up on their way.

Well, Vern and Charlie engaged them in a very friendly discussion about the afterlife and all its pleasures and seemed fascinated by all that they were told, but it slowly became apparent that they were reluctant to act upon their stated desire and were in fact much more interested in acquiring an alcoholic beverage from one of their favorite watering holes, which, of course, they could now afford to enter, being recognized only by the other dead alcoholics taking up residence around the still incarnate drinkers.

Bruno and Lloyd went along for the ride, not out of any real interest, as they had seen this sort of thing before, but on the off chance that they might be able to shift these characters quickly and be done with it. But it was not to be and they experienced a typical few moments of the discarnates-in-a-bar performance, which usually means hours of standing around amiably chatting with the other dead drunks and waiting for one of the live ones to pass out, whereupon there begins a mighty struggle to see who can get into the body first for that brief but ineffable experience of stupor they have stupidly substituted for transcendence.

Interestingly enough, there was a church just down the block, and an evening service in progress. As it is not uncommon to have lifelong churchgoers shift to their favorite spot on passing, they stopped in to see what was what.

Sure enough there were two ladies still insisting on being old, despite some indications that they had passed some twenty years before. Lloyd and Bruno knelt down beside them, and merely as a way of getting attention, began to flirt.

Lloyd insists, despite our groans, that he opened with the cliché, "Do you gals come here often?" Bruno claims that having not quite heard him, he can neither confirm nor deny but says they were almost tut-tutted out of existence. But being the troopers that they are (more groans) they waited out the disapproval and escorted the keen parishioners to their favorite little park, where they deposited themselves on the assigned bench to watch the world go by.

After a suitable period of defrosting, the ladies proved to be almost friendly, as long as the discussion was kept to religious matters. Bruno says he felt a couple more visits would be in order, and making their farewells they moved on towards the nearest sports stadium to see what they might find, of course changing costumes on the way.

A game being in progress, there were more than a handful of discarnates absorbing, vampirelike, the thrills of the crowd's excitement as it surged and rippled around. Realizing that there was nothing to be done until the game was over, they fell to observing and discussing that seemingly age-old dispute amongst us rescue workers: Are the recently dead just stuck in the groove of their old habits, whether they be drinking, devotion, or sports, or are they addicted to the self-generating energy of crowds?

It's an intriguing enigma and one we entertain ourselves with often, in our version of what you would call "downtime." A classic "Which came first, the chicken or the egg?" argument, it can easily recede into itself, quickly taking its debaters into that formless but energy-filled void where all manifestations arise simultaneously and cannot be causally distinguished. Ultimately pointless, but still lots of fun.

Just like life itself, I say to the group, who respond with howls of what I presume to be disagreement. Bruno apologizes for raining on my parade and proceeds to describe their quick visit over to the stock exchange to see if there were any dead business junkies to retrieve. As one of their regular stops, the costume change was automatic. From easygoing middle-aged sports fans, they turned into stockbrokers at a cocktail party, ties and grins loosened.

They found a couple of the regulars talking over old times. Manifesting some champagne and glasses, they joined them. Before being drawn into a discussion about some perceived upcoming fiscal crisis, which they knew from experience could go on for hours, they excused themselves to tend to a new, and perhaps more promising, arrival.

A successful young broker had been stopped in midcareer by an unfortunate car accident occurring perhaps an hour before, and precipitating the coma from which he had unknowingly wandered. Bruno sensed this almost immediately.

Michael couldn't figure out how he'd gotten from the dinner party to here, but yes, he'd be glad to down some bubbly with the boys. And what were they doing here after hours? Didn't they get enough punishment during the day? Gluttons, Bruno joked, pouring him another.

Michael declared it the best goddamn champagne he had ever tasted. How much did they fork over for this? He called out to the other two, who waved back amiably. Bruno steered the party chatter back to the dinner, casually asking first about the entrée and the wine and then the state of the highway traffic. It was then Michael remembered his accident.

"My God, you guys are angels, right? Gonna give me the tour? My wife told me all about it. But where's the tunnel with the light at the end? Cancelled due to lack of interest?"

It was then that Bruno noticed the guardian spirit standing behind him. He pointed him out to Michael and suggested this was his man. Michael, seemingly enjoying this game more by the minute, turned and shook his hand. And with a brief farewell they were gone.

They walked back to the other two and asked them if they wanted to move on to the great brokerage in the sky. No, they said, but we'll take a look around if you don't mind.

And that was all they needed, according to Lloyd. Ensconced in a reception-area hotel for those who consider themselves a cut above, they soon fell into conversation with some recently deceased executives whose reputations had preceded them. Puffed up with self-importance to be sure, but as Lloyd says, everyone's puffed up with something, be it pride, piety, or low self-esteem. I react: "They're all hurdles to be overcome, aren't they?"

Sunil returns out of nowhere and smirks, "That's not even a good line, never mind a best one."

Charity asks him about the conference seductions he was so concerned about. "Well, Sheila's out at the last minute with the flu and Emil's already got someone in bed. Not the one he's after, but he's just warming up."

Charity sighs. Her romantic sensibilities often seem offended by the manipulations of Sunil's crew. They cheat at the game of love and she just doesn't like it. But we've discussed it all before and I know she doesn't care to bring it up again.

Lloyd adds that we're all consummate liars anyway, but it's all in a good cause, isn't it? This, as you might expect, brings a round of chuckles, for we all know how true it is. It's the essence of our craft and art: conning people into coming with us and using any ruse that comes to hand. Julia insists we're just like mothers trying to coax recalcitrant children into bed, every night using another bait. I ask Sunil if that's the best line; he grins and shrugs.

Julia asks about the two church ladies—did they ever hustle them successfully? Lloyd says they're working on it. But he will say this: They're both a bit guilty over the back-street abortions of their careless youth and family-splitting arguments with children, and that is basically what's keeping them in fear of their fate.

Bruno wants to get back to their sports fans. After the excitement of the game had subsided, they returned to find small groups of fans discussing the game with that oh-so-familiar fervor: gesticulating hands and eruptions of laughter. Slipping into the periphery of a group, Bruno took a gap in the chatter to announce an all-star game in Heaven, if anyone wanted to come along.

Chamber Music in Your Own Home

Right then the string quartet showed up and I had to excuse myself from the group and show them to my recital room at the back of the cottage. I keep it there so as not to spoil the traditional image. But it's a beauty even if I say so myself. It had always been one of my unrealized Earthly ambitions to have enough space and influence to hire musicians for chamber concerts. I think it was reading one writer's fantasy of a period re-creation of Bach's Brandenburg Concertos in the original coffeehouse atmosphere that planted the seed all those years ago.

Well I've made good on my threats: Chamber recitals of both ancient and modern music are a staple of my social life. And my incarnations as a soiree and salon hostess have not gone to waste. Costumes are de rigueur at these sessions, and believe me, people still love to dress up. You fashion plates down there have no cause for worry.

We're setting things up around the grand piano when the clarinet and flute players arrive and I busy myself with introductions. The string players I've known for a long time, but the woodwinds, a husband and wife plucked from life while trying to change a flat on the highway, are quite new to the astral and are still buzzing with excitement.

New pieces by Stravinsky and Debussy, and neither of them really believed in an afterlife at all! It's all too much for two-bit players from a community orchestra. They thank me profusely for the opportunity. I tell them they're very welcome and turn to see Jurgen float in horizontally and come to rest lying on the piano. A whiz kid with attitude to spare, Jurgen would be nineteen if he were still alive and kicking, but a taste for wine and fast cars delivered him here before he'd even graduated from the conservatory. Not that he gives a toss. One plane, another plane, it's all the same to him.

I can imagine the saddened and disappointed parents he left behind, not to mention teachers, agents, and managers, but for him it's all just water under the bridge. He never cared for a career, he says, he lived for the moment, and music, cars, and wine gave ample opportunity for that. I can imagine what his guide's going to be telling him before his next spin about the globe, but it's none of my business. For me he's just a great pianist and I'm very pleased to have him here.

Jurgen, of course, takes that for granted and proceeds to float underneath the piano and back up over the top, arms folded like some smug corpse. Soon he has the other musicians in stitches and I see my chance to change and get ready for my guests. Whipping up several bottles of imaginary wine does not take as long as you might have imagined and most guests enjoy bringing their own goodies along. People can get very inventive with tarts and the like, let me tell you.

What does take some effort, at least for me, is deciding what to wear. "Costumes from across the centuries and cultures" is usually the theme of my musical soirees, and as they tend to attract the type who've explored both the gory and the glory in their lives, almost anything can, and usually does, appear.

I decide, more or less on a whim, to go as Henry, the no-account accountant, varying the standard-issue dark suit only with a lemon shirt and a broad salmon tie with matching carnation. A round of applause from my group of guides greets my reappearance. I bathe in my momentary glory.

Sunil seems to have taken up the slack in my absence with some priest-in-purgatory stories. As he is mainly concerned with sexuality and power issues, this is a natural for him. The sexual abuse of children has landed many a dead priest in what he thinks is Purgatory, and as the belief system is as ironclad as any I've come across, they will reside in that gloomy sphere until someone convinces them they're suitable Heaven material.

Some stay for weeks, others years, others decades. It depends on how depraved their behavior has been and how much they wish to punish themselves for it. Having attempted to live by a strict moral code, they are all the more harsh on themselves when the time comes for all to be laid bare.

Silent, remorseful contemplation in bare stone huts set in unforgivingly rugged mountain landscapes is often the sentence to be carried out. Sunil likes to drop by from time to time and get them to talk about sex, that terrifying taboo they've danced around for many lives, either thinking that its denial would bring them closer to God or its indulgence a defiant confirmation of their awful sinfulness.

He favors the blunt approach and often sits down to tell a few dirty jokes. If they raise a chuckle he knows he's on the right track, for humor, as we know, is the yolk in the cosmic egg. Often, unfortunately, they do not, and he sees the uphill struggle the two of them will trudge. That's if he's allowed back. Some prefer to suffer in isolation, feeling no doubt that is their due, and summarily forbid him to reenter their lives.

Sunil continues as I get up to greet the first of my guests. They make quite a pair: One is dressed, so he tells me, exactly like Jimi Hendrix for the 1970 Isle of Wight festival, and the other is the rotund, middle-aged version of George Frideric Handel at the height of his eighteenth-century London success. The rest of the crowd gradually appear in all shapes and sizes, a detailed description of which could easily take a couple of chapters. Imagine every period drama you've ever seen and blend elements from each into a transhistorical, cross-cultural cocktail that a planet on a bender would drink.

We stand around flirting and sipping wine and getting reacquainted. You can overhear lines like "God, I've haven't seen you since the Middle Ages!" and "Remember when we got burned at the stake?" and "Industrial revolution my ass! Waste of bloody time! Skipped the whole thing!" or "Just got back from Jupiter, amazing planet!" And of course, being the astral plane, there's always a few "Seen God yet? Get any answers that make sense?" followed by much raucous laughter.

If you are wondering about astral plane cocktail chatter that's as boring as its Earthly counterpart, then yes, it exists, as does almost everything else you can imagine, but not at my parties, where conventional behavior is definitely discouraged. I had enough of that on Earth, and most of it my own fault, I might add. Now I go for the eccentrics and iconoclasts.

And for that I have to thank Jack, my golfing buddy guide, who in my early days out here dragged me kicking and screaming out of my shell of proper behavior and showed me the joys of making it up as you go along. Simply put, without Jack I'd still be Henry. And this book, among other things, would not exist.

And if that makes you curious about where you'll be in the afterlife, take a look at where you are now, because unless you're fortunate enough to have someone like Jack, your most prominent characteristics and tendencies will most likely be replicated in your new environment.

The timid will be timid; the pious will be pious; the jovial will be jovial; the vengeful will be vengeful; the loving, loving; the fearful, fearful; the confused, confused; the angry, angry; the morose, morose. The gift of eternal life does not change people, it merely magnifies what is already there.

And I might add to that list: music lovers. There will be music lovers here. For despite the fancy costumes, that is who gathers here.

And although at this level there is no savage beast to soothe, we can all remember incarnations when there was such a beast.

Jurgen begins with a piano solo, a composition by a favorite of his, Chick Corea. It's a wonderfully brilliant and lyrical piece that seems to cascade endlessly, throwing up gorgeous swathes of color in fabulous abstract weaves. When he finishes and says, "I wish Prokofiev were here to hear that," some wag offers to go fetch him.

That's another thing about the astral: A lot of the historically famous people still here now prefer the quiet life and actively resist public exposure. Keep that in mind if you decide to look for one of your favorites.

Next we have a new (well, new to me) string quartet by Claude Debussy. Its progress is slow, more textures than melodies, and makes me think of an old man shuffling in his slippers towards nowhere in particular. After the exuberant energy of the Corea piece, the strings instill a calm that covers the room. Its energies seem simultaneously sensual and contemplative, moving more than a few listeners into mental plane territory, which is, I suspect, its intention.

When the players finish, we stand and bow. It's a ritual I've tried to encourage during my current stay on this plane, and as the magic of music more directly affects both the heart and mind on this plane, it is a reflex that arises quite naturally.

This leads to mingling and banter, the character of which I leave you to divine for yourself. When we settle down to the septet by Stravinsky we find we have energized ourselves to just the right level for a mad whirl of intermingling rhythms and melodies as all seven instruments seem to constantly ricochet off each other like subatomic particles laughingly eluding definition.

In contrast to the fine lines and ordered imagery created by the Debussy piece, this scintillating jangle of Stravinsky's manufactures a sparkling tapestrylike abstraction that invites the viewer to enter and get lost. Both the music and the images retain the seductive complexity of a maze, and many of us find ourselves wandering delightedly therein.

Another silent standing bow, and we are sadly released from the shaman's spell into the more ordinary magic of friendly chatter, during which I discover that Guinevere and Rachel have been here all along, quite to my surprise as Guinevere's taste in music runs more to renaissance and baroque than anything modern.

I am so delighted to be kissed on either cheek by the two of them, I can easily overlook their complaints of dizziness and confusion. They have both come as raven-haired pre-Raphaelite beauties, hair color being no more of a problem here than anything else. Think it and it is.

As my guests dwindle and finally disappear, we clear up the mess as quickly as we do anything else here, by a brief and concentrated effort of will. We do not marvel, as you might, when the unwanted disappears, for it is the natural condition of this plane; we just take it for granted, as you will do when you get here.

Guinevere senses that I have already spilled the beans on our intimacies, but as she had already agreed to her participation in the project, she remains mute on that count but insists that I draw a curtain across the time that she and Rachel and I will spend together.

Thus it is that I bring you forward to my next assignment with Gordon, "the author," which is, as promised, a vision of that plane where all one's incarnations can be viewed simultaneously.

All Time Is Now

Since Gordon was last with us so many pages ago, I would remind you that only one day has passed in his life, and that the accumulation of projected thought-form pictures of my divagations will hover in the psychic atmosphere of his home for the next few months until he finds time to write about them. And hopefully that paradox will serve to whet your appetite for what is about to come.

I am waiting for him beneath our favorite willow tree when I feel you readers will be requesting an update on my Romeo and Juliet suicide couple. Well, they have not come to any decision, but I suspect in the near "future" they will, although it is by no means guaranteed.

I can, however, visit them in a possible "future" and relate that outcome for you. It will take but a moment to sink "inside" and secure a projection.

Glenn has put a call out for me. Fortunately, I'm not too busy and can put in an appearance. They already look a little older and more dignified. Their infatuated focus on one another has reached some kind of saturation point and they are ready to reach out.

Helen insists that I see her flying abilities and proudly displays any number of stunts. I tell her I can see she's been practicing and she just hoots. I glance at Glenn; he grins proudly, almost like the father he imagines. After some more shenanigans we settle down to talk.

There's been some family visits during sleep time which have only been partially successful. Glenn's father in particular resents his disobedience. Helen's elder sister wants to have her as a baby and is distraught that Helen won't play along: She's happy in Heaven, thank you very much. Helen's parents seem the most forgiving: That God has taken their little girl seems only to have increased their faith. There's a purpose there, even if they don't know what it is.

Unfortunately this blind faith irritates Helen even more than it did on Earth. When I try to calm her and suggest a more tolerant approach, I can see she's in no mood to be trifled with. This battle with the pious parents has probably been raging for centuries one way and another.

I let her open up about the adoption scenario, which I can sense is why I'm really here. They've been too shy to ask anyone else, nervous that they'll be told they're too young and irresponsible. As you can see it often takes quite a while to shed Earthly mindsets.

They've been thinking over what I said, you see, and they're wondering if I could take them to one of these homes and show them around. I tell them no problem, just hold my hand and we'll be there in a jiffy.

And sure enough, there we are, walking along a path through a lawn area dotted with bushes and swarming with children. It's a sort of cross between a summer picnic and elementary school recess. Nobody pays the slightest attention to us.

I lead Glenn and Helen through the gardens to the other side of the building, which could easily pass for some sprawling mansion in Westchester County. Suddenly, we're beside a small flock of women and toddlers. There's a paddling pool and a fountain spilling into a duck-filled pond. (I have long since gotten over my paranoia about telepathic ducks, you'll be pleased to know.) On the far side of this grassy patio are the sliding glass doors that I know will reveal a roomful of babies and mothers.

Helen is smitten almost immediately. My friend Grace appears, baby in arms and, sensing my mission, places it directly onto Helen's arms. Grace and I move aside, pretending to have things to catch up on. It doesn't take long until Glenn is wiping away Helen's tears and then holding the child himself while Helen collapses into Grace's arms.

I think you can guess the rest. But just remember: that's but one of several possible scenarios. Just as on Earth, nothing is cast in stone. Anything could happen: They could even decide to reincarnate as brother and sister or the classic inseparable twins. And yes, you're right, such choices might be counterproductive in the long run, but if souls are determined, no advice can dissuade them. Advisers can be, and often are, ignored. Hell, if guides were always listened to, there'd be hardly any bad karma left to work on.

Well, Gordon's here now, and he's full of talk about what was, for him, "last night." He says he barely recalled a thing in the morning, but for a series of mysterious images concerning an old car swirling in a muddy river and someone sitting on the bank upset.

Then he saw the papers, with the front pages filled with disaster news. That's what he'd been up to! He spent the rest of the day thinking it over and taking a few notes when he got the chance.

Of course, now that he's back here with me, it's a different story. He now remembers how useless he was. I tell him it was not so bad for his first major disaster. A little steeling of the nerve and he'll be better next time. He wonders how I can be so blasé about it all. I tell him I've seen it all before. I'm not any different from any other astral helper; I know that disasters are merely mass open-air transitions. Everybody gets to where they're going eventually.

That seems to settle him, and he's on my case about tonight's project. First of all, I cloak him in a sort of protective vibrational shield, basically so he'll remain more or less conscious throughout. Then we do some meditation, aligning ourselves as best we can with the high vibration we're about to enter. Then we go.

Hand in hand we ascend, me constantly feeding Gordon energy of a highly refined nature in the hopes that he'll be able to cope with the intensity of the experience. The constant risk is that he will just pass out from an overdose of ecstasy, leaving me not only as facilitator but also as sole witness, with the unenviable task of channeling the experience to his incarnate self later on.

The reward will be twofold. First, for Gordon, an understanding of how all his lives are indissolubly linked not only to each other but also to the evolution of the planet itself and all the life-forms on it. Second, the opportunity to communicate this understanding to a widespread audience.

And who will be organizing this display, I hear you asking. Well, my impression, which is generally reliable but certainly not infallible, is that our higher selves, those lovely translucent onions I was describing earlier, since they dwell on that level which is the first energy step-down from the God level and thus have almost unlimited powers, are the motive force behind this display.

Imagine about twenty large television sets suspended in front of you in two tiers. Now feel a fabulously comfortable armchair underneath you with a small control panel by your fingers, which you somehow know how to work. Have you been here before? It all seems vaguely familiar.

You press a button and all the screens come to life. You are, as Gordon is, fascinated. I am watching him watching in case he forgets half of what he sees. As an Earth-bound movie buff I know he likes the setup. Of course, he's had more lives than twenty, so these will be the significant turning-point ones. The pointless repeats and biding time ones are usually left out.

Starting on the bottom left he sees a baby swaddled in animal skins, sleeping by an open fire in what could be a cave. The fire fades, then dies. The baby wakes, then cries. No one else seems to be around.

To the right is an image of a middle-aged man, again dressed in animal skins. Standing in a river, he appears to be spearing fish. When he takes his catch home, several happy children dance about him as his wife builds a fire.

Next we see what seem to be two brothers building a house from large rocks unearthed in a nearby field. The land is virtually treeless and definitely not equatorial. As their seemingly endless back-breaking work continues, we notice the next screen displaying a domestic dispute.

Around a rough-hewn kitchen table two men frown and gesture. The furnishings and clothes suggest mid-nineteenth-century America. We tune into the dialogue: Yes, it's just before the Civil War. Slavery is the issue. Small children cower in a corner. A brawl begins but is brought to a halt by a woman waving a shotgun. Tragedy seems inevitable. A struggle over the gun triggers the death of one of the cowering children, and we look at the other three screens to see, (a) the lone baby eaten by wolves, (b) the happy fisherman, surrounded by sleeping children and engaged in merry intercourse with his wife, and (c) the two brothers on their deathbeds, sharing some disease.

Gordon glances over at me, grinning. I return the favor, glad he's taking it so well. The top left screen, which has so far been freeze-framed, erupts into movement, if you call a nun bent in prayer movement. Next to her a nurse attends to wounded soldiers by lamplight. To the right of that we see a pretty girl raped behind a darkened building. She strikes her assailant with a hidden blade. Next we glimpse an aristocratic lady entertaining her lover in what could only be called, in its sumptuousness, a boudoir. Like a cheap farce, the husband enters on cue, and as he stabs the naked lover we see he is also the rapist from the previous screen. We return to the nurse, who lies abed praying for peace. The nun appears withdrawn in silent meditation, her darkened cell a haven from all activity.

Another woman, in some half-collapsed shack, dies in agonizing childbirth, her other two children looking on, appalled. We see them living with what appears to be an aunt, slaving at her whim. As teenagers they escape her cruelty, only to die in some plague. Screen right we see a happy couple, weavers by the look of it, adjourning from their work for a simple supper with two chattering children. England before the Industrial Revolution.

In order to simulate the all-at-once nature of these incarnations, the screens display their narratives in rapid-fire mode. There's a well-dressed boy, lying by a brook in the long grass, obviously daydreaming. There's a woman at her wedding, the crowd solid and self-satisfied in a middle-class merchant sort of way. We see her later, slightly pregnant, taking lessons on the harpsichord. Another woman, her hair and manner wild, paints small canvases in what looks like a drafty attic with a dirty skylight. Another shelves books in a large library. Another, either born into or cast into poverty, gives herself to strangers in darkened alleys for pennies. The self-hatred is stunning.

Back on the bottom row there's a couple of warriors, one at the peak of his physique, trouncing his enemies without any trouble, the other young and headstrong, an arrow in the heart at twenty.

Next to these a couple of sedentary intellectuals. The first some kind of minister studying a Bible, the second more like a philosopher debating with his gentlemen friends at dinner. We see the man of God defending himself in some kind of ecclesiastical court and failing. Whatever the issues, they're important to him, and he returns home completely disaffected with his church. The philosopher dies old and contented, blessing all who surround him with his innate goodwill.

On the female line there appear two scenes of women in distress. One sits in a castle bedroom, all stone walls and thick drapes, very pregnant and very lonely. Another stands on the seashore, shawl drawn about her shoulders, pining toward the horizon. One is wealthy, the other poor, but both are learning that loneliness knows no class bounds. One has only a demanding father-in-law, who thinks a weekly rape is his due and her solace, the other no father figure at all, only old women in a time of war. Both turn to their young sons for sustenance, starting lifelong obsessions that stunt everyone's growth.

Gordon seems to be taking this all in like the dedicated moviegoer he is. Frankly, it's all a bit much for me. For despite all my adventures, here, there, and everywhere, this is something I've never fully addressed. I know, you're shocked, an old hand like me. Gordon was shocked too. He couldn't understand why I wasn't just desperate to experience it. I told him that's what life is like here: far too much to do and not nearly enough bodies to do it in.

Just as I'm registering these thoughts I notice him slumping: Yes, he's flaked out from too much stimulation. I carry him back to my place and lay him down underneath the willow, where he will come to in his own good time. I lie back and listen to the birds. But not for long: I find myself wondering about Reid and Fiona, so I skip down to their level and take a quick look. Fiona's friend Deborah smiles at my approach. Guess what, she tells me, they've gone to the Riviera. I shake my head. That Reid always was a ladies' man. I'm surprised Fiona fell for it. Deborah and I share a chuckle and I'm off.

Gordon seems to be stirring. He looks groggy and amazed. "That was incredible," he says. "I was every one of those people and none of it really mattered! All that pain and anguish and here I am, up for more? It's all too much."

I suggest splitting up into three or four personalities and incarnating into the same time frame in different countries. After he dies this time, of course. Wouldn't want to rush things, would we?

Fortunately, he sees the funny side of it. I ask him how he sees himself now. He closes his eyes and says, after a moment: "As blindness given sight, as a planet given people, as dimension given fragrance."

"As dimension given fragrance? That's a bit much, even for you." I'm always teasing him about his writing; he takes it so seriously. He assures me it'll look great on paper.

We discuss the possibility of his remembering tonight's vision well enough to write it all down. He says he'll try. He says that every time, and almost every time he forgets nine-tenths of the whole, and I have to do all the image projections from here, aiming them at his apartment so he can pick them up in the months to come.

Still, I shouldn't complain: It was my idea in the first place.

Afterword

Over the centuries, mystics, occultists, magicians, Rosicrucians, theosophists, Sufis, shamans—virtually anyone you care to slot into the esoteric student category—have devised a variety of maps and coordinates to describe their experience of the worlds beyond the body. And except for the last two hundred years, repressive Big Religion made sure they all operated as secret societies. As such, their various jargons were a useful deterrent to the prospect of snoops: Their codes of secrets kept them private, if not exactly safe.

I came of age studying spiritualism and theosophy, so terms like astral, mental, and buddhic plane mean a lot to me. And although I am comfortable with terms like chakra, etheric, astral, and antahkarana, I realize others may not be. You may have come to this work from any of several directions. Today we're faced with a mess of terms invented by more modern teachers.

Robert Monroe, especially, feeling antsy about excessive subservience to tradition, invented a system of focus levels. His years of experiment suggested to him that the levels of consciousness could be divvied up into at least 27 focus levels, with levels one through 21 being physical and those beyond 21 being non-physical. So many people have been to The Monroe Institute that he founded in Virginia that his system of focus levels seems to have taken on a life of its own. (Roughly, the lower astral is equivalent to focus 23 and 24, the mid-astral to focus 25 and 26, and the upper astral/lower mental is equivalent to focus 27.)

Many students, overwhelmed with the obvious utility and efficiency of his Hemi-Sync tapes in assisting consciousness shifts, seem to never quite realize that Life Before Monroe did, in fact, include retrievals and explorations under other names. Theosophist Charles Leadbeater's 1896 *Invisible Helpers* contains several examples of OBE rescues and astral assistance very similar to the type of thing described by Robert Monroe and Bruce Moen. Lord Hugh Dowding, chief of the Royal Air Force during World War II, operated, with his wife and friends, a spiritualist rescue circle, retrieving lost souls from the area Monroe would term focus 23. The accounts of their work in *Lychgate* (1945) sound like many a retrieval that I and others did in the Iraq War of 2003. With this in mind, I would suggest we are contributing to a tradition, not creating one.

Each level is defined by the fears and desires of the inhabitants. They move on as they, one by one, drop their fears and desires. In some places they don't care about God; in other places they're angry about God; in others they want to know more about this God concept; in others they like arguing about God; in others they're asleep, waiting for judgment day; in others they wonder where the heck his representatives are; in others they love him madly and praise him endlessly. There are plenty of levels beyond, but to unleash that at this early stage would be counterproductive. Suffice it to say that little spheres of light are where it's at.

It has been my experience that each plane shades imperceptibly into the next, and that there are so many subplanes as to be not really worth counting. You might as well ask how many churches there are in America: obviously lots, and they've all got a slightly different take on theology. The important thing to learn is how not to get stuck, either by your own fear and desire, or by rules imposed by others, and how to travel without prejudice or impediment. Henry knows, I know, and hopefully these books will help you to know.

About the Author

Gordon Phinn was born in Glasgow, Scotland, in October 1952 and educated at Glasgow Academy. He moved to Toronto, Canada, after the death of his father in March 1968.

About 1970, his discovery of popular spiritualist books such as *Life in the World Unseen* by Anthony Borgia helped him to put into perspective certain haunting dreams in which his father would say, "Try to imagine I've gone on a long holiday." Further readings in spiritualism, theosophy, and the Western esoteric tradition slowly expanded his understanding of the Mysteries, leading to such modern teachers as Gurdjieff, Krishnamurti, Seth, and David Spangler.

His interest in the mystic and esoteric bred a fascination with the entire range of paranormal phenomena. He studied the world of researchers, psychics, healers, and channelers without ever imagining he might become one himself.

In the late 1990s, his lifetime of sporadic lucid dreams exploded into a four-month extravaganza of near-nightly adventures throughout the planes with a variety of guides, of whom Henry seemed to be the ringleader. After the usual anxieties of the "what will people think?" variety, he plunged into the narrative which has become *Eternal Life and How to Enjoy It*.

Hampton Roads Publishing Company

. . . for the evolving human spirit

Hampton Roads Publishing Company
publishes books on a variety of subjects,
including metaphysics, health,
visionary fiction, and other related topics.

For a copy of our latest catalog, call toll-free
(800) 766-8009, or send your name and address to:

Hampton Roads Publishing Company, Inc.
1125 Stoney Ridge Road
Charlottesville, VA 22902

e-mail: hrpc@hrpub.com
www.hrpub.com